FRANCESCO MATTESINI

DISASTER AT TOBRUK

THE PLANNING OF THE BRITISH "DAFFODIL" AND "AGREEMENT" OPERATIONS

AUTHOR

Francesco Mattesini, born in Arezzo (Italy) on April 14, 1936. He moved to Rome in July 1951. He served, as civilian employee, at the Italian Army General Staff, 4th Department, from 1959 to 2000. Collaborator of the Historical Offices of the Italian Military Navy and the Air Force Historical Office, for which 20 books and about 6'0 essays were produced. He is currently retired, always living in Rome.

LICENSES COMMONS

This book may utilize part of material marked with license creative commons 3.0 or 4.0 (CC BY 4.0), (CC BY-ND 4.0), (CC BY-SA 4.0) or (CCO 1.0). We give appropriate attribution credit and indicate if change were made in the acknowledgements field. All our books utilize only fonts licensed under the SIL Open Font License or other free use license.

Related all the British navy or RAF image of the book the expiry of Crown Copyrights applies worldwide because: It is photograph taken prior to 1 June 1957 and/or It was published prior to 1970 and/or It is an artistic work other than a photograph or engraving (e.g. a painting) which was created prior to 1970.
For a complete list of Soldiershop titles please contact Luca Cristini Editore on our website: www.soldiershop.com or www.cristinieditore.com. E-mail: info@soldiershop.com

DISASTER AT TOBRUK - the planning of the British "Daffodil" and "Agreement" operations
Di Francesco Mattesini. A cura di Luca Cristini. ISBN code: 97888932726283
Prima edizione agosto 2020   Code.: **SPS-066 EN**   Cover & Art Design: Luca S. Cristini & Anna Cristini

STORIA is a trademark of Luca Cristini Editore, via Orio 35/4 - 24050 Zanica (BG) ITALY. www.soldiershop.com

DISASTER AT TOBRUK

THE PLANNING OF THE BRITISH "DAFFODIL" AND "AGREEMENT" OPERATIONS

DI FRANCESCO MATTESINI

SUMMARY

Planning of the "Agreement" operation..Pag. 5

The tasks assigned to the various units involved in the "Daffodil" operation.....................Pag. 13

The movements of the British Naval Forces and the predictions of the Axis Commands..Pag. 21

The start of the British attack on Tobruk..Pag. 27

The failure of British motor torpedoes to force the entrance to the port of Tobruk......Pag. 41

The sinking of the destroyer SIKH..Pag. 45

The Axis Air Force's attacks..Pag. 63

The cryptographic information of the Ultra organization..Pag. 91

The "Hyacinty" Operation: the attack by the LRDG on Barce airport........................Pag. 95

The failure of the "Bigamy" and "Nicety" operations to attack the port and airports of Benghazi and conquer the Gialo oasis..Pag. 103

The "Anglo" operation: the attack by the saboteurs of the Special Boat Section on Rhodes airports on the night of September 13-14th 1942..Pag. 111

Supermarina's considerations..Pag. 115

Conclusions..Pag. 123

PLANNING OF THE "AGREEMENT" OPERATION

After the overwhelming land offensive of the Axis forces in Egypt, which began on May 24th, 1942 in Ain el-Gazala (Cyrenaica) and then, after the conquest of Tobruk on June 20th, up to the fatal dunes of El Alamein (50 km to west of Alexandria), in early August the British military commands of the Middle East studied how to ease the pressure of the Axis on the front. And then force Field Marshal Erwin Rommel, commander of the Italian-German Armored Army, to detach part of his forces elsewhere facing the 8th Army of General Bernard Montgomery, who assumed command on the 13th of the month[1].

Thus was born the "Agreement" operation, on a plan conceived by Lieutenant Colonel John Edward Haselden, commander of the "Long Ranger Desert Group" (LRDG), the department specialized in sabotage and coups operations in the desert. Established in 1940 The "Agreement" was part of a more complex series of other operations, called "Big Party", intended to provoke upheaval, panic, disservices and destruction of the Axis logistic organizations, by means of in-depth actions of spoilers, destined to act against airports, logistics centers and Cyrenaica land lines, between Tobruk and Benghazi[2].

In the "Big Party" the most important operation was undoubtedly the "Daffodil", to be carried out against Tobruk, to destroy the installations and deposits of the port, the most important port of supply from Cyrenaica from Italy and Greece. But equally important were the "Bigamy" operations (Snowdrop) to destroy the Benghazi fuel depots and attack the Benina airport; "Haycinth" (Caravan) to destroy military installations at Barce airport, as well as the statue of Benito Mussolini; and "Nicety" (Tulip) to conquer the Gialo oasis for the time necessary to cover, by land, the retreat of the various rates of saboteurs engaged in the aforementioned operations.

The planning of the "Agreement" was discussed by the Middle East Command, in Cairo, under the direction of General Claude Auchinleck, who had signaled to his headquarters *"that to achieve that purpose it would have been justified to employ any means[3]"*. But shortly thereafter, the replacement of Auchinleck, confirmed by the British Prime Minister Winston Churchill, who reproached him for a slightly aggressive demeanor, was confirmed, and in his stead he was destined, as by the new commander of the Middle East, General Harold Alexander. The "Daffodil" operation involved an attack from the sea side on the Tobruk stronghold, coordinated with the action of a terrestrial mobile column coming from the desert on trucks. However, it raised a lot of perplexity among the commanders of the Mediterranean Fleet and the RAF, Admiral Henry Harwood and air marshal Arthur Tedder, because

---

1 The Joint Planning Staff of the Middle East presented a proposal on the attack on Benghazi and Tobruk on August 3, 1942. The rational part for both actions was summarized in: *"The enemy depends almost entirely on Tobruk and Benghazi for its supplies for the area of El Alamein, with the exception of about 300 tons per day at most in Matruh: all the ships and port facilities of Tobruk and Benghazi can be destroyed, this could lead to the rapid defeat of Rommel by land forces"*. The project also established which forces were to be employed in the action, and how these should operate. In conclusion, the document stated: *"The destruction of the gasoline installation in both ports, more particularly in Tobruk, the night seriously embarrasses the enemy. The extent to which he would perform the enemy's operation will depend on our ability to sink tankers in the port. We must be prepared to accept the loss of some naval forces, along with many of the people taking part in the operation"*. See Peter C. Smith, Massacre at Tobruk, William Kimber, London, 1987, pp. 33-35.

2 Stephen Roskill, *The War at Sea 1939-1945, vol. II, The period of balance*, London, HMSO, 1956, p. 309.

3 It must be said that the idea of carrying out an action on Tobruk had already been put forward for some time in the face of the difficulties encountered by General Auchinleck on the El Alamein front, so much so that the British Admiralty had proposed to send *"a destroyer to bomb Tobruk all dawn after an enemy convoy arrived in that port"*. The aforementioned hunt was intended for sacrifice. The Commander of the Mediterranean Fleet, Admiral Henry Harwood, *"wanted the landing of the war unit to be followed by a landing on the coast to cut Rommel's supply lines. His idea prevailed over that of fellow commanders who believed the raid [of the destroyer only] too bloody and difficult to succeed"*. See, Michael Carver, The battle of El Alamein ", Baldini & Castoldi, Milan, 1964, pp. 129-130.

in fact the raid of the "Daffodil" had modalities *"whose unquestionable audacity of execution"* was *"equal only to the cumbersome and also to the naivety of the plan"*, which was accepted by the three commanders in chief of the British armed forces of the Middle East and then issued on August 21st, 1942[4]. It consisted of a surprise attack, ready to be implemented in the months of July and August, and then postponed to the night between September 13th and 14th (Sunday and Monday), to take advantage of the favorable moon phase.

The "Daffodil" operation was to lead to occupy Tobruk, starting from the landing, for about twenty-three hours, to allow departments of troublemakers, according to the time available (it was believed twelve hours) for the complete destruction (Demolition Party) of the port facilities and naval units: barges and special vessels at anchor in the harbor, minus ten motor rafts, the most efficient to catch and which were to be used to transport the prisoners captured in the raid and to reinforce the landing craft in Alexandria. The destruction of all the logistics and warehouses of the stronghold was added, in particular the bomb-proof tanks containing Rommel's petrol stocks, and also of the tank repair shops[5]. In this way it was intended to paralyze the efficiency of the stronghold, as a port and supply base and the possibility of movement of the Italian-German armies, for a long time[6].

The British naval historian captain Stephen Roskill, in the second volume in his monumental work *"The War at Sea"*, wrote that by means of destroyers there was the intention to land the marines on the northern ridge of the Tobruk harbor while the troops transported from the coastal units they would have landed on the southern ridge of the bay in support of a terrestrial column *"coming from the desert"*.

▲ On the left, Lieutenant Colonel John Edward ("Jock") Haselden, creator of the Plan Agreement, who died in Tobruk on September 14th, 1942. He was born in Egypt to a British father and a Polish-Italian mother. On the right, General Harold Alexander, commander in chief of the Middle East.

---

4 Mario Montanari, *Operations in Northern Africa*, vol. II, El Alamein, Rome, Army General Staff - Historic Office (from now on SMEUS), 1989, p. 640
5 AUSMM, "Maricolleg Berlin, English plan for the landing in Tobruk (13-14 September 1942)", Germanic Navy in Italy
6 S.O. Playfair, *Mediterranean and Middle East*, vol. IV, The Destruction of the Axis Forces in Africa, London, HMSO, 1980, p. 20

▲ Admiral Henry Harwood, commander-in-chief of the Mediterranean Fleet at the center of the picture. He was famous for the combat sustained in December 1939 off the Rio della Plata, when with three light cruisers he faced the German battleship Admiral Graf Spee, forcing it, damaged, to enter the port of Montevideo, where it sank itself.

▼ Air Marshal Arthur Tedder, Commander-in-Chief of the Middle East RAF.

After neutralizing the coastal defenses with artillery fire, the destroyers had to enter the port, and *"protected from the enemy artillery positions"* that were to be captured and manned - destroy the *"ship's equipment and then re-embark the marines and the soldiers"*.

However, faced with the reality of carrying out an operation born with too much presumption and little consideration for the reaction capabilities of the defenders of Tobruk, Italian and German, Roskill added that *"a frontal assault with such very weak forces certainly now appears excessively risky"*[7]. If the "Daffodil" operation had succeeded, it would have had very serious consequences for the trend of the Axis supply sea traffic, also because most of them made a stopover in Tobruk, the port closest to the front, and from Tobruk also the traffic of the motor rafts that transported tanks and supplies to Marsa Matruk started, and in the middle of the beach even beyond as close as possible to the line of the land front of El Alamein. A possible interruption of even a few days would have forced the Axis convoys to forward maritime supplies to the port of Benghazi, which was 260 miles further back, and therefore it was necessary to transport vehicles and supplies for the only land route, the coastal road Balbo, which was subject to continuous air strikes, especially with fighter bombers, while bombers mainly beat ports and airports.

Though, there were still many doubts about carrying out the Agreement operation. Indeed, General Alexander wrote in his report[8]: *"Since the actions would have certainly been very risky, the advantages that they wanted to derive from them had to be carefully weighed with the probability of success and the price of any failure. As a result, on September 3rd, I once again reviewed the project together with Admiral Harwood, Commander-in-Chief in the Mediterranean, and Air Marshal Tedder, Commander-in-Chief of the Middle East Air Force. At that time, the fighting was in full swing in El Alamein. Two weeks of fighting food was all that the enemy had managed to accumulate for his offensive, and although there was not much hope of irreparably damaging the ports, even a temporary impediment to supplies in addition to the failure of the offensive - now granted - could have been disastrous for Rommel's army. Even if the actions were unsuccessful, they would no doubt have had some effect on the enemy's morale and would also have induced him to take all precautions against future such actions on our part by distracting forces from defending positions in Egypt"*.

Marshal Tedder pointed out that in any case it would not have been possible to provide any air support except for an attack by bombers, to protect the forces employed in the approach phase to Tobruk, while for the distance the protection of the fighter was absolutely impossible. Admiral Harwood, commander of the Mediterranean Fleet, realized that all the landing force, including two destroyers that he proposed to employ, could very well have been lost, but accepted the risk. In the end it was considered that the results of the operation would be such as to justify the risks connected to it, and orders were consequently given for the actions to be carried out on the basis of the plans prepared[9].

Admiral Harwood's concerns were more than justified, considering the strong defense existing in Tobruk. There were in fact four coastal batteries of the Royal Navy, some batteries of the Royal Army and twelve anti-aircraft batteries, six of them German with 88 mm cannons and as many Italians of the 1st Group of the Maritime Artillery Militia with cannons of various caliber. According to some sources, 17 anti-aircraft and coastal batteries were present in the stronghold and along the coast, including 78 pieces of artillery, of which 48 were Italian and 30 German.

---

7 Stephen Roskill, *The War at Sea 1939-1945, Vol. II, The period of balance*, cit., pp. 309-310.
8 Harold. Alexander, *"The African Campaign from El Alamein to Tunis, from 10th August 1942 to 13th May 1943"*, Supplement to the London Gazette del 13th Feb. 1948.
9 Winston Churchill was made aware of the final details of the "Agreement" series of operations on September 11th, 1942, two days before the start of naval and land movements, with an immediate ciphered message from the Commander-in-Chief of the Mediterranean Flet. 11301C at 2.00 pm) sent to the First Lord of the Sea Admiral Dudley Pound to be delivered to the Prime Minister, in which he concluded with: *"It is believed that all operations have a reasonable chance of success, and that participation in the game is small compared to the results that could prove substantial"*. See National Archives, ADM 223/565.

▲ Italian M 41 tanks disembarked in an Egyptian port from a raft left from Tobruk in the summer of 1942.

▲ August 1942. The British leaders of the El Alamein front. At the sides of Prime Minister Winston Churchill: Marshal Harold Alexander on the left and General Berhard Montgomery on the right.

▼ Tobruk in the summer of 1942. Steamships, rafts and other vessels at the quayside and at anchor in the harbour.

Then there were, on the Italian side, 3 batteries with a 20 mm machine gun, and 13 coastal defense batteries with 47 47 mm anti-tank guns. However, these forces, in part of the 2nd Anti-Aircraft Artillery Regiment of the Royal Army, were considered insufficient for their splitting, having to defend an extension of coast of about 20 km.

Admiral Harwood later described the planning of the "Agreement" operation as "*a desperate undertaking*", as it arose from an urgent request for help from the 8th Army, and was justified only by the uncertain situation existing at that time on the El Alamein front. Situation that, in fact, had become particularly dangerous at the end of August, when General Rommel attacked on the southern front of the British deployment, in Alam el Halfa, but without being able to achieve the expected objectives, namely the circumvention of the enemy front from the south , because the offensive, announced by the British cryptographic source Ultra, was adequately thwarted by General Montgomery's 8th Army, and ended in two days due to the inferiority of the Axis vehicles; especially of planes and fuel (naphtha and petrol), since only a few transport ships from Italy managed at that time to overcome the British air-naval blockade[10].

Two groups of light naval units called Force A and Force C were assigned to embark most of the British troops destined for the "Daffodil" operation, which we remember was the part of the "Agreement" plan concerning exclusively the Tobruk objective. Two large "Tribal" class destroyers of the 22nd Squadron were assigned to Force A: the Sikh, with the commander of the squadron and the expedition, ship captain St. John Aldrich Micklethwait, and the Zulu of the frigate captain Richard Taylor White.

▲ Three MTBs in high speed navigation

---

10 Thanks to the interceptions and decryptions of the British cryptographic organization Ultra, which revealed objectives and forces committed by the Italian-German Armored Army, including the number of tanks, the new commander of the British 8th Army, General Bernhard Montgomery, who possessed slightly higher than those of the opponent, with the exception of the aviation which instead was clearly superior to that of the Axis, inflicted on Rommel's forces a hard defeat of arrest at Alam el Halfa, on the southern front of El Alamein, frustrating the intention of Field Marshal to reach the Nile Valley and the Suez Canal. Rommel's tactic, developed stubbornly with inadequate forces, and with the usual now known maneuver of going around from the south in a restricted area like that of El Alamein, was what the enemy expected; and was cleverly confronted by Montgomery engaging, rather than its mass of armored forces (935 tanks of which 713 efficient) spared as much as possible, a wall of anti-tank and field guns, perfectly camouflaged, and successfully used in an advantageous position on the heights to slow and then break the advance of the Italian-German tanks, which took place, also having to cross extensive minefields, for about 45 Km. before returning to the starting bases. Everything was then surrounded by the incessant attacks of the Anglo-American air force, which caused Italians and Germans a large part of the human and vehicle losses. The balance of the losses reported by the two adversaries in the battle of Alam el Halfa was as follows: Germans: 1859 men among the dead, injured and missing, 38 wagons, 33 cannons, 298 vehicles, 36 planes; Italians: 1,051 dead, wounded and missing men, 11 wagons, 22 cannons, 97 vehicles, 5 planes; British: 1,750 men killed, injured and missing, 67 wagons, 15 anti-tank guns, 68 aircraft.

The two units carried, under the command of Lieutenant Colonel E.H.M. Unwin, 380 marines of the 11th battalion of the 2nd Royal Marines brigade, to which were added a detachment of anti-aircraft artillery and coastal defense, a subsection of the 295th field company of the genius and a detachment of signaling, all embarked in Haifa, Palestine. Each of the two destroyers carried six boats with Ford engines and nine boats destined to be towed from the previous ones at the time of landing. In total, to bring the soldiers of Force A ashore, there were twelve motor boats, and eighteen towing boats, all rudimentary and flat-bottomed, built in Egypt with seasoned wood, on board the Sikh and the Zulu. Force C, in Alexandria, included sixteen torpedo boats, seven from the 10th Flotilla (MTB 260, 261, 262, 265, 266, 267, 268) under the command of frigate captain Robert Alexander Allen, and nine from the 15th Flotilla (MTB 307, 308, 309, 310, 311, 312, 314, 315, 316) under the command of the frigate captain Denis Jermain. The latter, aboard MTB 309, was also the commander of all torpedo bombs. Then there were the three ML 349, 352 and 353 motolances.

The nineteen small units carried about two hundred men, stationed in a company of the Argyll and Sutherland Highlander regiment, 1st machine gun platoon of the Royal Northumberland Fusiliers, two motorcycle sections of the 295th field company of the genius, a detachment of anti-aircraft artillery, a detachment army and a detachment health service.

Ten soldiers were transported aboard each torpedo boat, while the motolances embarked a particular department of forty navy pilots and specialists (including sixteen officers), with charges and demolition vehicles, under the command of the corvette captain Nichols. To command Force C, which sailing at 6.00 pm on September 12th was to proceed to Tobruk in a single formation, was destined instead the captain of vessel John Fulford Blackburn, former commander of the famous river gunnery Ladibyrd at the time of his sinking in Tobruk, on May 12th, 1941 for attack by German bombers Ju 88 of the 8th Squadron of the 3rd Group of the 1st Experimental Squadron (8./LG.1), dependent on the Air Command Africa (Fliegerführer Afrika).

▲ Captain Denis Jermain, commander in the attack on Tobruk of the 15th Torpedo Flotilla (MBT), and the torpedo boat group.

THE TASKS ASSIGNED TO THE VARIOUS UNITS INVOLVED IN THE "DAFFODIL" OPERATION

The landing operation, as mentioned, was to begin on the morning of September 14th, taking advantage of the dark hours and the lack of moon. The tasks assigned to the various units and departments involved in the "Daffodil" operation were to neutralize the coastal defenses of the stronghold and the enemy artillery positions of Tobruk, after an aerial preparation of the RAF, assigned to the 204th Group (deputy marshal of the air Arthur Coningham) with heavy and medium bombers, which lasted all night to force the garrison to remain in the shelters for as long as possible[11].

The destroyers and torpedo-torpedoes of Forces A and C would then intervene to carry out, with a coordinated action from land and sea, the destruction of the various facilities of the port, torpedoing all the ships that were in the harbor, the docks and piers, fuel depots, artillery, workshops and port facilities, and to recover the men who had been involved in the sabotage operation at the end of the action. The Sikh and Zulu were to be guided to the point fixed for the landing of the troops, in Marsa Sciaush in the northern ridge of the Tobruk peninsula, on a stretch of coast with very uniform morphology, which would have been indicated to the two Force A destroyers by the landed signalers from the submarine Taku (Force E). After the disembarkation of a first rate of troops, the barges, motor and trailer, which transported the soldiers and their armament, had to return to the two destroyers to embark and bring the other soldiers to the ground, completing the disembarkation around 03.00. So, dividing to attack the assigned targets, the entire 380 marines contingent of the 11th Battalion had to head south to the bay of Tobruk, to occupy the town and the port. After the landing of the troops, the Sikh and the Zulu had to go to cross towards the west, and at the signal of the green light (after the destruction of the anti-ship batteries transmitted by the troops on the ground) around 08.00 enter the harbor. Attacks were also planned by the RAF command of the Middle East to attack the departure airports of the German bombers Ju 87 and Ju 88 in North Africa and Crete, if the available air forces had allowed it, and to provide protection with escort of fighter planes to naval groups both on the outward and on the return from Tobruk with the aircraft 201st Air-naval cooperation group, including the long-range twin-engine fighters Beaufighter of the 252nd and 272th Squadrons. At the same time, the one hundred and fifty soldiers transported by the fifteen Force C torpedo-bombers were to take land on the southern ridge of the same peninsula, inside the Tobruk roadstead, and then head south to occupy the town and the port. To support the amphibious operation, a terrestrial column of eighty-three men had to intervene, starting with eighteen modified 3-ton Chevrolet Canadian trucks, from the Libyan oasis of Cufra, located 700 miles south of Tobruk, conquered by the soldiers of the Free France of the General Leclerc in March 1941 and remained in British hands who used it to carry out their commando actions[12].

---

[11] Among the many diversions to facilitate the action on Tobruk, there was one on Siwa ("Coastguard" operation), with the intention of attracting the attention of the enemy aviation, with a fake airfield at the oasis, simulated with the throwing of dummies that were traps, as they destroyed themselves. These mannequins (which were then used also in the Normandy landings) were launched on Siwa during the night of 13/14th September, and the following morning there was a movement of ground troops (1 SDF bds) which was transferred to the oasis of Babarya towards Siwa, to then return to Barbarya the next day 15th. The diversion took place without incident, and according to the report of the operation, the enemy was made to believe that Siwa could be attacked and that it was necessary to reinforce it, as in fact it happened after detaching an Italian armored personnel carrier.

[12] The oasis of Cufra, in southern Cyrenaica on the border with Egypt and 1,600 kilometers from Cairo, constituted the main advanced base of the LRDG, and its garrison in September 1942 was formed by troops of the Sudan Defense Force and by detachments of the regiment Welch. To reach it from Egypt, to the British, troops and supplies, it was necessary to cross a very long stretch of desert, partly sandy, partly gravelly, advancing along the Nile to Asyut and then for a rudimentary track to the oasis of el-Dakhla, and before arriving in Cufra it was necessary to get around the red sandstone cliff of Gilf el-Kebir. This entailed enormous effort in transfers for men and means.

The column, named Force B, had moved from Cairo to Cufra on August 22nd, and under the command of the same creator of the Agreement plan, Lieutenant Colonel Haselden, had the following task[13]: *to enter the fortified perimeter of Tobruk at sunset on the initial day of the action, disguised as a column of prisoners of war, and at 20:30 reach behind Marsa Sciausc; at 20:45 the attack on the batteries and defenses of the area was to begin, to constitute the landing head of Force C. The patrol of the L.R.D.G. he had to enter the perimeter two hours later (presumably after the alarm) in the meantime destroying the Radiogoniometric Station and possibly acting against the landing fields of Gubi.*

To accomplish this feat, the men had to approach the eastern side of Tobruk aboard seven trucks camouflaged with the colors and insignia of the Afrika Korps, the palm and the swastika, and the men supplied with falsified documents in Cairo, and with weapons hidden under some blankets but always to be kept close at hand.

Force B was made up of: a detachment of the SS (Special Service) Brigade under the command of Major Colin Campbell and with the men disguised as British prisoners of war, with their weapons hidden; a detachment of anti-aircraft artillery and coastal defense; a section of the 295th field company of the genius; a signaling detachment; a detachment health service with a doctor; a patrol of Long Range Desert Group (LRDG) commanded by Captain Davd Lloyd Owen and used, for the specialization in long-range desert operations, to pilot the column of the other troops. Finally, under the command of Captain Herbert Cecil A. Buck, there was a detachment, known as the Special Interrogation Group (SIG), made up of six Palestinian Jews of German origin who, wearing German uniforms, were to make it appear that they were supervising the prisoner soldiers, to then approach the landing area of Force C with them to facilitate the task. If they had been taken alive they would have been lucky if they had been shot immediately on the spot[14].

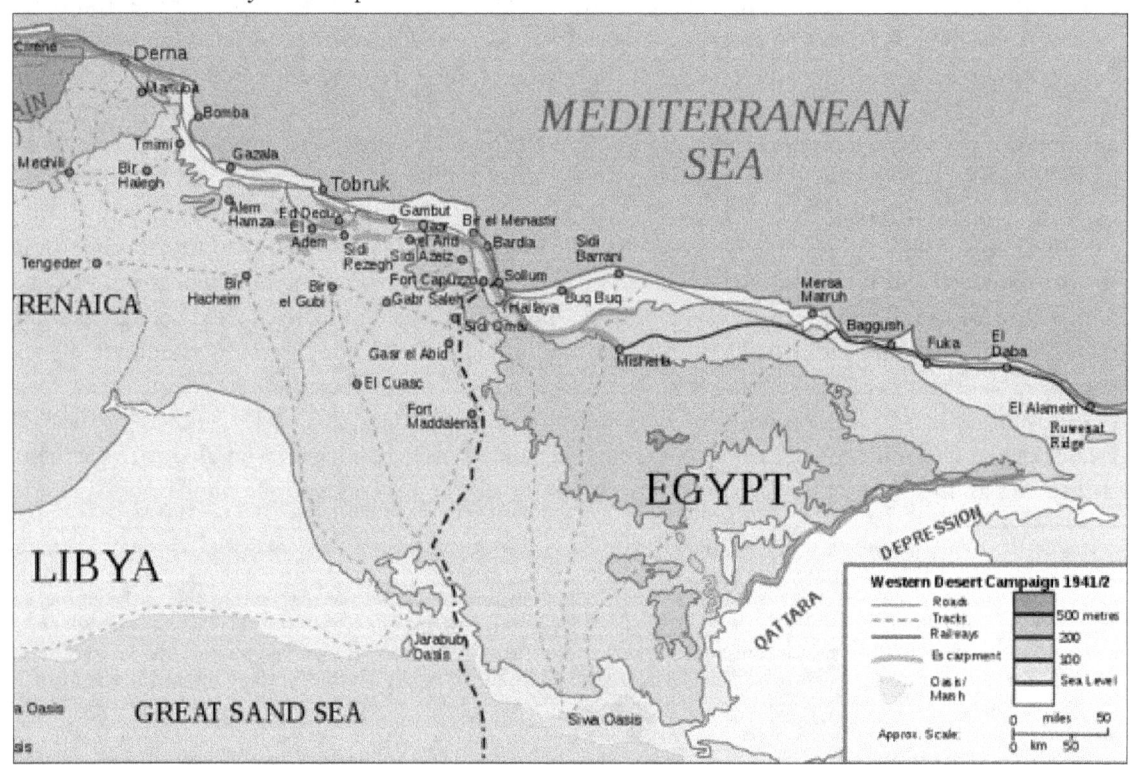

▲ Eastern Libia and Western Egypt

---

13 AUSMM, "*Supermarina, Enemy operation against Tobruk and Cyrenaica rear, 14th September 1942-XX* ", Naval clashes and war operations, file 91.
14 R.P. Livingstone, "The great forays into the desert ", *History of the Second World War*, vol. 3, Milano, Rizzoli-Purnell, 1967, p. 310.

▲ Seven Commando officers at Hatiet Etla: Lieutenant John Poynton, Major Colin Campbell, Lieutenant Michael Duffy, Lieutenant Graham Taylor, Lieutenant David Sillito, Lieutenant Mike Roberts (or possibly Lieutenant Ronald Kirk) and Lieutenant Bill McDonald.

▼ LRDG captain David Lloyd Owen.

The men of Force B should have headed towards the town of Tobruk along the southern coast of the bay, until they occupied Marsa Sciausc, from where they could facilitate the landing of Force C troops on the point provided with luminous signals.

Along the march to reach the goal, and subsequently, they also had to destroy plants and posts and anti-ship batteries on the southern ridge of the Tobruk peninsula, in particular the two Italian batteries of the coastal defense, one of the Royal Army and the other of the Regia Marina.

The transport demolition departments of the three Force C motolances did not have to participate in this first phase of the operations. In fact, according to the "Agreement" plan (CC (42) / 72) of August 21st 1942, found by the Italians on September 15th on a stranded landing craft, their task was as follows[15]: *The motolance with the spoilers had to stay close to the coast, near Marsa Sciausc, without taking part in the actions, until around 08:00, time at which the free entry to the harbor was foreseen: then they had to enter the port and destroy all the boats after having selected ten efficient motor rafts to be captured, armed and sent to Alexandria after embarking on them of Italian prisoners, any English prisoners freed, injured and loot material.* Different was the task that was assigned to the torpedo boats, in that after the landing of the troops in Marsa Sciausc, they had to force the obstructions of the roadstead when the ground departments would reach the docks of the port, to start the planned destruction work of plants, deposits and ships.

▲ German Jews of the Special Interrogation Group (SIG).

---

15 AUSMM, "Supermarina, Operazione nemica contro Tobruk e retrovie della Cirenaica, 14 Settembre 1942-XX", *Scontri navali e operazioni di guerra*, cartella 91

Ultimately, in the complex Agreement planning, compiled by examining the British operational order, Forces A, B and C had to carry out: *Occupation of Tobruk for about 24 hours in order to operate the total destruction of the port facilities and anchorage units, as well as all the preparations and logistic depots, so as to paralyze for a long time the efficiency of Tobruk as a port and supply base. In case of favorable developments in the general situation, instead of returning by sea, Forces A - B - C had to head eastwards by land, operating in correlation with Force X, further paralyzing the supplies towards the front (and probably acting on the back of the our deployment during the enemy offensive in Alamein).*

With regard to the withdrawal from Tobruk, the "Agreement" plan specified[16]: *All forces were expected to leave Tobruk the evening after landing, returning - in principle - by sea, to the units of Forces A and C, and to the ten captured motor rafts. In the event of complete success, some of the forces had to return by land, on captured vehicles, operating - in connection with Force X - against our lines of communication. Any missing men would have been collected three nights later by a submarine in Marsa Scegga near Bardia.*

All documents, including the fundamental operational order of the "Agreement" operation, which in Tobruk, as mentioned, fell into the hands of the Italians who immediately informed the Germans, bore the indication "Secret" not to be brought into combat "; provision that was violated, because evidently individual commanders needed to consult them in their minute, rigid and long-winded form. If the soldiers were captured, the soldiers had been advised to keep silent; if they had been interrogated, they had been told to indicate the way to the retreat of Bir El Gobi, while the troops would have had to fall back to the oasis of Gialo, if necessary, during the movements to wide range in Cyrenaica, task assigned to Force X in the "Bigamy" operation.

About these operations in the Cyrenaic desert, in the Supermarina report it is written: *"Force X was to operate for about three weeks (likely duration of the offensive at Alamein) in the hinterland of Benghazi and Derna, in order to paralyze any supplies to the east: for Force X had to rely on Gialo as a logistic base for these operations"*. With the "Nicety" operation, Gialo's oasis had to be occupied *"with Force Z, coming from Kufra. The duration of the occupation had to be extended for about three weeks, in order to use the oasis as a logistic base for Force X"*.

According to the same order of operation, the British estimated *"that the garrison of Tobruk was made up of fewer than a regiment of poorly performing Italian soldiers and groups of German specialists, in addition to the armaments of the batteries[17]"*.

In assessing which Axis forces were in the Tobruk area, it was believed that[18]: *The Tobruk garrison includes about 1 Italian infantry brigade and numerous staff of the c.a. About 1000 German soldiers accased 24 km. east of Tobruk but probably that they do not have the necessary means of transport to immediately take action. However, it must be counted that these troops may intervene later. Tobruk's artillery defense includes 8 coastal pieces, 48 pieces c.a. heavy and 85 pieces c.a. light. It is assumed that 30 Macchi 200 are located in Tobruk and El Aden airports. Some 88 and Me 110 as well as 24 Italian torpedo bombers must be located in Derna. It must be counted that a group of 30 Ju 87s from Sidi Barrani may intervene within an hour. The intervention of a second group is likely within 3 hours. Ju 1 from Crete can intervene within 1 ½ hours. Within a few hours 130 enemy planes can take action. The action will be initiated by an airstrike against Tobruk on the D1 / D2 night.* [13/14th September].

Finally, in the order of operation for Company B of the 11th Royal Marines Battalion (Major John Norman Hedley), of a particularly cynical and ruthless character, sent for information to the commander of the battalion Lieutenant Colonel Edward Harold Mitford, it was specified that the

---

16 Ibidem.
17 Stato Maggiore Esercito Ufficio Storico (from now on SMEUS), *Diario Storico del Comando Supremo*, vol. VIII, tomo II, Allegati, Roma, 1999, p. 69.
18 AUSMM, Maricolleg Berlino "Piano inglese per lo sbarco a Tobruk (13-14 settembre 1942)", Prot. N. 608/S. Le informazioni fatte pervenire a Roma dall'Ammiraglio di Collegamento con l'Alto Comando della Marina Germanica, ammiraglio Giuseppe Bertoldi, erano stati ricavati dai tedeschi dalla consultazione del piano britannico catturato dagli italiani, e mandato in copia a Berlino.

10 Platoon, in attacking and conquering a deep shelter assigned after having circumvented it, had to detach a section to kill all the men who were there, and therefore without taking prisoners. And he specified: *"Once the task is completed, the 10th platoon will reach the Battalion command at full speed in the predetermined place[19]"*.

The captured Agreement plan was later brought to the attention of Supermarina and a copy to the German Navy Command in Italy.

The latter on behalf of the command in chief of the Kriegsmarine, great admiral Erich Raeder, thanked Admiral Arturo Riccardi, Chief of Staff of the Royal Navy, on October 20th, asking to have a photocopy of the document available[20].

▲ OperationAgreement. The oasis of Kufra in August 1942. Men swim in the lake.

---

19 AUSMM, "Comando Supremo, Documento catturato al nemico", *Scontri navali e operazioni di guerra*, cartella 91. Major Hadley and Lieutenant Colonel Unwin were captured on September 14th and sent to Italy by air.
20 AUSMM, "Supermarina, Operazione nemica contro Tobruk e retrovie della Cirenaica, 14 Settembre 1942-XX", *Scontri navali e operazioni di guerra*, cartella 91.

▲ The commandos, crossing the desert, head by truck towards the oasis of Kufra.

▲ Soldiers digging to get a truck out of the soft sand on September 6th. In the foreground, with a Scottish Kilt, Major Colin Campbell, second in command of Kufra's party.

▼ The trucks stopped on the huge rock spur of Gilf Kebir. The officer with the binoculars is most likely Major David Lloyd Owen.

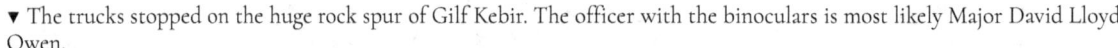

THE MOVEMENTS OF THE BRITISH NAVAL FORCES AND THE PREDICTIONS OF THE AXIS COMMANDS

The nineteen light units of Force C took the sea from Alexandria at 6:00 pm on September 12th, and headed in formation towards the west, at a speed of 8 knots, and then increased it, by order of the captain of vessel Blackburn, to 24 knots. During navigation, the MTB 268 torpedo-torpedo boat (second lieutenant of vessel. David Cowley Souter), due to an engine failure, after transferring his ten soldiers to the ML 353 motorboat, was forced to reverse course to return to Alessandria.
The two Force A team destroyers, Sikh and Zulu, also sailed from Haifa at 6:00 pm on September 12th, and joined with a support group.
In fact, to give the landing naval support, at 19:45 of that same evening the units of Force D sailed from Port Said, consisting of the anti-aircraft cruiser Coventry (captain of vessel Ronald John Robert Dendy) and the four escort destroyers of the type "Hunt" of the 5th Flotilla, Belvoir, Dulverton, Hursley and Croome. To this group were added the Sikh and the Zulu, at 05:45 on September 13th.
A second naval group, with the four escort destroyers of the 5th Hurworth, Beaufort, Exmoor and Aldenham Flotilla, set sail from Alexandria at 09:25 on September 13th and also rejoined Force D west of Alexandria, north of Abukir Bay, and then continue to the west at a speed of about 25 knots, with the ships frequently changing course, proceeding zigzagging, to dodge the attacks of any submarines. So, after the Sikh and Zulu had left Force D at nightfall heading for Tobruk at a speed of 30 knots to carry out the "Commando" operation, Coventry and the eight escort destroyers remained to cross offshore Marsa Matruh, with the task of remaining in the area for strategic naval protection, and to resume the return route on the morning of the day following the landing, September 14th.
At the same time, another British naval group, consisting of the light cruiser Dido (vessel captain Henry William Urquhart McCall), of the 15th Division, and the five team destroyers of the 14th Jervis Flotilla (vessel captain Albert Lawrence Poland), Javelin, Pakenham, Paladin and Kelvin, carried out

▲ The MTB 268 (ex USS PT 19), which due to an engine failure after leaving Alexandria was forced to return to port.

the "MG 7". That is, a diversion to the main operation "Agreement" with the Dido which bombed the coastal town of El Daba, west of El Alamein, starting from 01:00 on the 14th for thirty minutes. The cruiser fired three hundred and fifty 133mm bullets, half of which were believed to have fallen on the target. The entire naval force, at 3:30 pm, returned to Port Said without incident. The Middle East Royal Air Force (RAF) (Air Marshal Arthur Tedder) was expected to provide naval groups with air escort on both outward and return journeys, particularly with the 252° long-range Bristol Beaufighter fighters and 272° Squadron of the 201° Group, particularly trained in this task, which involved flying long and long distances over the sea.

While the torpedo-boats and motolances of Forces A and C in approaching the target followed an isolated route, the Sikh and the Zulu, after being accompanied until sunset by the anti-aircraft cruiser Coventry and by the eight escort destroyers (who then remained to cross north of Marsa Matruh assuming indirect protection to the operation "Daffodil"), with the favor of the night they decidedly headed towards Tobruk. The British movement did not go unnoticed, since between 08:30 and 08:35 on September 13th German reconnaissance aircraft Ju 88D of squadron 2. (F) / 123 of the X Fliegerkorps, referred to on the directive of April 21st 1942 of the O.B.S. (Oberkommando Süd) competed for the offshore reconnaissance in the Eastern Mediterranean, after taking off from Skaramanga (Crete) they signaled two groups of ships; the first of six war units about 15 miles north of Rosetta, at the mouth of the Nile (Force D), and the second of two steamships with four escort units 12 miles north of Alexandria.

The contact with the group, after the initial sighting, was not maintained, nor was any other indication received. Therefore, since the routes of the two naval groups were erroneously reported on the east, during day 13th, also due to the poor visibility conditions that hindered the reconnaissance, the sighting did not provoke any provision until 18:20.

▲ The cruiser Dido. At the bow of the bridge six 133 mm high elevation cannons in twin turrets, particularly effective in anti-aircraft firing. Another four 133mm cannons in two twin towers were located aft.

▲ The light cruiser Coventry (4290 tds), dating back to the First World War, having entered service on the 21st of February 1918, resumed after modernisation and conversion into an anti-aircraft vessel in the second half of the 1930s. It was armed with eight 102 mm cannons in individual, unshielded, installations.

▼ The escort destroyer Croome, one of eight units of the "Hunt" class of the 5th Flotilla of the D Force. It was armed with six cannons in 102mm twin towers, and had no torpedo launchers.

▲ The disembarkation jacks of St. Mark's Battalion were in Tobruk. In the picture below, the men of the 1st Company in combat dress, commanded by Lieutenant Bernardini.

At that time the OBS Command, which was then Field Marshal Albert Kesselring Commander in Chief of the South German Front (Oberbefehlshaber Sud) and at the same time of the 2nd Air Fleet (Luftflotte 2.) with tactical headquarters in Taormina, corrected the direction British units, which included torpedo boats, pointing out that their route was to be understood as west and not east. However, since this verification, carried out after more than ten hours from the two sightings, was not accompanied by any observation, the various Axis commands, believing that the specification of the O.B.S. could have *"a purely cartolary value"*, did not have the feeling that the enemy naval units were focusing on the coastal areas of Cyrenaica, and believed that they should not exceed the Marsa Matruch meridian during the day. Therefore Supermarina, the operational body of the General Staff of the Royal Navy, believed that the group had not gone further west and that the morning sighting referred to a local operation. Consequently, there was a complete lack of any warning warning of likely enemy actions to the local Italian-German garrisons, *"and therefore the first operations against Tobruk could take place completely by surprise"*[21].

The Chief of Staff of the Royal Navy, team admiral Luigi Sansonetti, who was informed of the landing in Tobruk only at 02:00 on September 14th, complained of this in Rome for the possibility of probable enemy actions, and then received, at 03:35, the news that against that important base had been *"launched a violent airstrike"*, while *"there was still no precise information on the outcome of the landing"*[22].

However, noting that the bombing, which began at 20:30 on September 13th, had an intensity and duration greater than that of the previous raids, so much so that it continued uninterruptedly until 02:40 and then continued with the only machine gunning until 03:15, in Supermarina the doubt arose that the airstrike intended to cover some port forcing action or some action against coast targets[23].

Only at 09:00 the news sent by the OBB that *"the landing had failed"* reached Rome, and that the enemy ships were heading west, leaving behind two burning units.

If, during the day, Supermarina had confirmed the enemy movement to the west, if it had been authorized by the Chief of Supreme Command (Stamage), Marshal Ugo Cavallero, and therefore through him also by the Duce (Benito Mussolini), it would have been possible to order the 8th Division, kept ready in Navarino (western Greece), to take the sea.

On the morning of the 14th the Naval Division would have been in an excellent position to act against the residual enemy groups. The lack of air reporting therefore resulted in the loss of a very favorable opportunity.

Admiral Sansonetti regretted that by telephoning the team admiral Angelo Iachino, Commander of the Naval Squad in Taranto at 10:45 on September 14th, he claimed that due to the disservice of the aerial reconnaissance, the three cruisers of the 8th naval division (Giuseppe Garibaldi, Duke of Abruzzi and Duke of Aosta (located in Navarino with five destroyers of the 13th Squadron) to be able to find themselves at 06:00 of that day *"in a very favorable position"* to attack the enemy, after a navigation journey 320 miles. In the letter n. 25458, sent to the Supreme Command on September 19th, from the subject *"English landing in Tobruk on September 14th"*, Admiral Arturo Riccardi, Undersecretary of State and Chief of Staff of the Royal Navy, made the following clarifications[24]: *The enemy group that carried out the landing operation in Tobruk on the night of the current 14th, was spotted around 08:30 on day 13th in*

---

21 AUSMM, "Supermarina, Operazione nemica contro Tobruk e retrovie della Cirenaica, 14 Settembre 1942-XX", *Scontri navali e operazioni di guerra*, cartella 91.
22 *Ibidem*
23 According to the German War Diary of the Seetransportstelle (Office of Maritime Transport), on September 14th there were the following eight merchant ships in the Tobruk harbour: Ostia, Sybilla, Ankara, Iseo, Kreta, Milthiades, Johannis Kutofari, Cornelli II.
24 AUSMM, *Scontri navali e operazioni di guerra*, b. 91.

the Alexandria area, and at the moment signaled en route to the east. Only around 18:00 O.B.S. he specified that it was to be understood en route to the west. The contact with the group, after the initial sighting, was not maintained, nor any other indication was received, while during the day the enemy had to sail at least to the Marsa Matruch meridian. Therefore Supermarina believed that the group had not gone further west and that the morning sighting referred to a local operation. If, during the day, there had been confirmation of the enemy movement to the west, the VIII Division would have been ordered, ready in Navarino, to take the sea. On the morning of the 14th our Division would have been in an excellent position to act against the residual enemy groups. The lack of air reporting therefore resulted in the loss of a very favorable opportunity.

▲ Part of the 8th Italian Naval Division in Navarino, Western Greece, in the summer of 1942. From below the cruiser Duca d'Aosta with the destroyer Bersagliere, and further on the cruiser Duca degli Abruzzi with the destroyer Mitragliere.

THE START OF THE BRITISH ATTACK ON TOBRUK

Let's see now how the British attack took place. After the sunset of September 13th, coming with the seven trucks from the oasis of Cufra, the men of Force B of Lieutenant Colonel Haselden, exploiting the German uniforms, stopped south of El Aden an Italian truck carrying a patrol of seven men of the Air Force, an officer, a non-commissioned officer, four airmen and a worker[25]. Then, after questioning them, two airmen were shot, one of whom was wounded and the other unharmed, abandoned on the ground because they were believed to be dead, returned on foot to Al Aden. Continuing the march, an officer killed an unsuspecting German sentry, with the usual devious system, and collecting his rifle as a trophy. General Giuseppe Mancinelli, at the time official Italian liaison with the command of Marshal Rommel, rightly deprecated the ruthless behavior of British soldiers, considered true bandits, against prisoners, citing how the elimination of the Italian patrol occurred, for having learned it from an airman who escaped the massacre[26]: *A truck with about ten of our soldiers was to perform some service at 15-20 km in the interior south of Tobruk, met a column of Germans (such as ours, they considered them) who got off and they stopped with the excuse of asking for information, then surrounded them, disarmed them and, after making them aligned, mowed them on the spot with a volley of machine guns. My interlocutor was saved because he fell unconscious, probably out of fright, before being reached by the total discharge and found himself unharmed under the bodies of the killed companions.* The men of the Royal Air Force massacred were: the second lieutenant Amleto Fortuna, the sergeant Antonio Petruccini, the airmen Antonio Pollastrini and Enzo Bisi, and the worker Alberto Pompili. The airmen Germano Serafini and Salvatore Esposito survived[27].

MOVEMENTS AND ATTACK DIRECTIONS OF THE BRITISH FORCES FOR THE ATTACK ON TOBRUK AND OTHER TARGETS OF THE CYRENAICA AXIS

To coincide with the beginning of the aerial bombing, at 9:30 pm the men of Colonel Haselden moved to enter undisturbed the perimeter of the Tobruk Square, their presence having escaped the terrestrial surveillance - deceiving the men of German vehicles met along the way - and aerial reconnaissance which, despite having flown over the column of vans, did not recognize them. In this way, the men of Force B, once they had easily passed the poorly guarded defensive perimeter, were able to separate and then destroy sheds and cornerstones with the launch of hand grenades, and upon reaching the locality of Marsa Sciausc, launch upwards towards the sea the prescribed very red and green signal flares. After which Haselden signaled the conventional word "Nigger" in Cairo, which was immediately retransmitted to Force C.

Six of the fifteen Force C torpedo boats left Alexandria were kept ready, and with a red light lamp it was provided by the lieutenant of the vessel. T.B. Langton, British Special Service officer, warned MTB 309 commander, Lt. Denis Jermain, that the road to enter Tobruk was clear[28]. However, following the ongoing airstrike, related to the repeated reporting of the presence of an enemy submarine in the coastal area immediately next to the entrance of the harbor (it was the Taku), the commander of Marina Tobruk, captain of Temistocle vessel believing that the conditions for commando actions or landings concomitant with the airstrike in the coastal area or against the port, d'Aloja had immediately given order to the lookout posts and motorboats to intensify coastal surveillance[29].

---

25 G. Santoro, *L'Aeronautica italiana nella seconda guerra mondiale*, vol. II, Milano - Roma, Edizioni Esse, 1957, p. 327.
26 Annotation by General Giuseppe Mancinelli, in the article by R.P. Livingstone, *"The great incursions into the desert"*, cit. p. 311
27 P. Caccia Dominioni, *El Alamein 1939-1962*, Milano, Longanesi & C., 1963, p. 244.
28 R.P. Livingstone, "The Great Incursions in the Desert", *History of World War II*, cit., pp. 310-311.
29 AUSMM, "Comando Marina Tobruk, Attacco nemico alla Piazza di Tobruk", Marilibia, cartella 15.

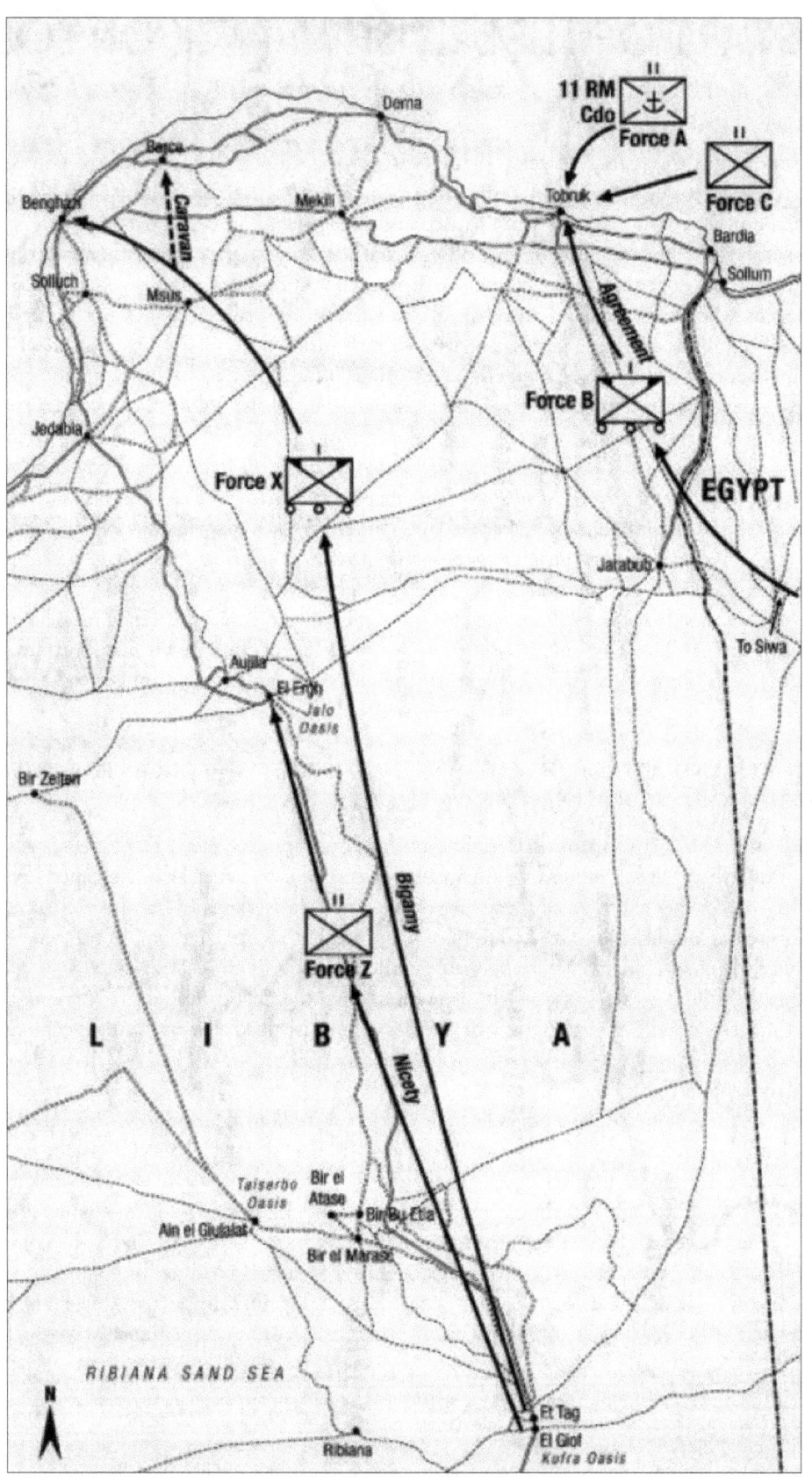

▲ Operation Agreement. Above, the Force B commando column in El Kharga. Notice the appearance of the men in the hellish summer heat of the Libyan desert. Below, during a stop at Hatiet Etla, Force B's vehicles are camouflaged with nets and sheltered by trees to hide them from the enemy's aerial exploration.

▲ Wellington of the 37th Squadron flying over the desert. This unit, part of the RAF's 205th Group, participated in the night bombardment of Tobruk.

▼ The MBT 309 (former US PT 51) where Lieutenant Denis Jermain, commander of the 15th Torpedo Flotilla (MBT) and the torpedo boat group, was in the attack on Tobruk.

At 01:05 on September 14th, a radio communication was intercepted by an isolated destroyer [Sikh] who claimed to be on the spot established for the start of the operation, and simultaneously occurred in Marsa Sciausc, east of the mouth of the harbor, the landing of British soldiers transported by torpedo boats[30].

Meanwhile, British air force attacks were increasing in intensity. The bombings had begun, in the light of illuminating flares, at 21:00 on the 13th, with a delay of half an hour on the order of operation, and ended at 03:15 with the machine-gun actions. For the bombing of Tobruk on the night of 13-14 September, the order of operations of the Command of the 205 Group of the RAF (deputy marshal of the air Aklan P. Ritchie) provided for the use of one hundred and three planes, of which the medium bombers Wellington of the Squadron 37°, 38°, 108° and 148°, the Liberaton heavy bomber (B 24) of the 160° Squadron, and the Halifax heavy bomber of the 227° and 462° Squadron (the latter Australian), which had just been constituted each with sixteen aircraft. But the planes actually participating in the mission were one hundred and one: sixty-seven Wellington, fourteen Halifax, and fifteen British Liberators (B 24), to which were added five US B 24s. Of all these bombers, three aircraft returned due to technical problems before reaching the goal, so ninety-eight planes arrived in Tobruk which beat the predetermined areas in successive waves even with large-caliber bombs, the 4,000-pound "blockbusters" (1,814 kilos) . In particular, the two Italian anti-ship batteries Dandolo, (four 120 mm cannons) and Tordo (three 102 mm cannons) located between Marsa Mreisa and the town of Tobruk (where the main landing of the Commandos was to take place) were targeted, while the five US B 24s of the 98th Group bombed the ships in port[31].

According to British crews, they were spotted on the Tobruk peninsula, in the area of heavily attacked artillery positions, and noticed several large fires and a large number of explosions, including one, probably of a 4,000 pound bomb, particularly violent near the naphtha tanks, followed by two strong fires.

During the operation, in which 70 tons of bombs were dropped, four Wellingtons, three from the 70th Squadron, that took off from Abu Sueir, and one from the 108th Squadron[32] were lost due to the damage reported in the large anti-aircraft reaction. The latter had taken off at 20:00 on September 13th from LG-237 airport, west of Cairo, and with pilot Lieutenant E.R. Wardley. Overall, according to a document from the Italian Supreme Command, the bombing began at 9:00 pm on September 13th and continued until 03:40 am on the 14th, for a duration of six hours and forty minutes. It was believed that about one hundred and fifty aircraft had participated with the release of over five hundred bombs[33].

According to what was reported by the British crews, the enemy anti-aircraft guns, believed to be twenty-four, fired effectively during the first hours of the operation, and then decreased in intensity becoming irregular as the attack developed.

---

30 In a German communication directed by a Cyrenaica Naval Command, at OBS (Kesselring), II Luftflotte (Loerzer), Panzer Army (Rommel) and German Naval Command (Weichold), and decrypted on the evening of September 14th by the British cryptographic organization Ultra, it reads: *"Urgent Immediate. At 02:10 a.m., 3 green pier, alarm signal, for the approach of enemy ship, enemy east landed at Tobruk in Umel Sciause, naval station W/T [radiotelegraphic] is ready for defense and destruction of confidential books"*. (ZIP/0139/14/9/42).

31 S.O. Playfair, *Mediterranean and Middle East*, vol. IV, The Destruction of the Axis Forces in Africa, cit., p. 22

32 Of the four Wellingtons who failed to return to base, part of the crew of one of them was captured, while three men who tried to reach the British lines were killed on September 18 in a firefight with an Axis patrol on the Sollum - Sidi Barrani road. Another aircraft made a forced landing during the return trip, and only two crewmen (who were heading towards El Alamein and met along the way a crew member of a 148th Squadron Wellinton that had crashed into the desert on the night of 19/20 September) managed to reach the British lines. The third Wellington lost an engine on the Tobruk target and had to land forcedly in the desert behind the Axis lines. The crew avoided capture until September 20th, when they became prisoners of war. The fourth Wellington sent a message indicating he had engine trouble and was forced to make a forced landing in the desert. The men of the crew survived but were captured. One of them died when the ship that was transporting him to Italy was torpedoed and sunk. See, Alun Granfield, Bomber over Sandand Snox: 205 Group RAF in World War II.

33 ASMEUS, *"Sintesi delle operazioni svoltesi in Cirenaica della notte da 13 al 19 settembre 1943 – XX"*.

▲ Halifax of the 462nd Australian Squadron (Egypt 1942) based in Fayid since September 7th, 1942, when the department was established. Before the attack on the night of September 13th, he had carried out two other raids on the target.

▼ Wellington of the RAF's 70th Squadron. In the night raid on Tobruk he lost three planes by Italian and German anti-aircraft.

▲ A B.24 of the 98th US Bombing Group crashed after landing without landing gear. The unit participated in the night bombardment of Tobruk and the ship in the port of Benghazi.

▼ Wellington crew of the 108th Squadron receive instructions for a mission from the commander. An aircraft from this unit was the only loss of the big night air raid on Tobruk by the anti-aircraft defending the base. The shooting down of the aircraft was included in the Supreme Command's War Bulletin.

The men from the last plane I left the target area reported that no more than three cannons were still firing intermittently. And to say in this regard that in those hours of the night the defense's attention was concentrated against the landing of the commandos under construction, and the objectives of the Italian-German artillery, those closest to the coast, were therefore represented by naval units. That same night, according to the plan to attack the airports of Crete and the Desert, that of Sidi Heneish (Haggag el Quesada), where many German departments were based, including the Bf 109 fighters of III./JG.27, the three groups of dive bombers Ju 87 of the St.G. 3 and Italian fighters Mc 202 of the 3rd Wing, was attacked by the average US bombers B 25 of the 12th bombing group (Colonel Charles Goodrich) based in Ismalia (airport LG-209), who with Squadrons 81st, 82nd, 83rd and 432nd made a total of sixty-six missions. But four B 25s were shot down by the anti-aircraft, which had an easy target in the dark, due to the opening of the room (compartment) of the aircraft bombs with the lights on.

Also on the night of September 13/14th, but in connection with the Bigamy operation, the attack by Earth on the Benghazi targets, winds between Liberator bombers of the 159th Squadron of the RAF and US B 24 of the 98th Group (343rd, 344th, 345th and 415th Squadriglia), commanded by Colonel Hugo P. Rush, taking off from Palestine airports, bombed the ships in the port. The raid took place between 20:45 and 01:00, but the results of the bombing could not be observed because the Benghazi targets were obscured by a cloud cover of 10 tenths. The crews of the aircraft only saw the fire from the enemy anti-aircraft artillery. Subsequently, during the day of September 14th, the B 24 of the 98th Group had the target of Suda, where following the bombing, a burning ship was seen in the harbor, while in reality the air attack did not lead to any success. At the same time that the night aerial bombardments were developing, the commandos of Force B, after reaching the southern beaches of the Tobruk peninsula, with a surprise hit they managed to take possession of an anti-landing battery of 105/28 mm cannons of the Italian Army , the n. 105, posted on the western edge of Marsa Sciausc, right in front of the wreck of the armored cruiser San Giorgio, who had sunk there by the crew in January 1941 when the British, having reason for a substantial Italian garrison, had entered Tobruk. *"The staff of this battery remained largely overwhelmed, but an officer, who escaped the opponent with two men, quickly reached a neighboring battery and managed to communicate the incident by telephone to the Colonel Interim Commander of the sector by 23:40"*, At his headquarters in Tobruk, the divisional admiral Giuseppe Lombardi, commander of Marina Libia (Marilibia), assumed the direction of operations, assisted by his chief of staff and commander of the port, captain of vessel Temistocle D'Aloja. With Colonel Battaglia present, they examined the situation that had arisen and made agreements for law enforcement, arranging[34]:

a) Immediate dispatch, by truck, of the Command core of the [3rd] Battalion S. Marco, to Marsa Umm Esc Sciausc, to face the enemy infiltration and regain the 105 mm battery;

b) the establishment at the Marine Command of a mixed mobile defense company, consisting of 40 sailors, 40 CC. RR. of the 18th Btg. and a platoon of 30 Germanic sailors who showed up to take orders;

c) the deployment of reinforcements on the docks of the port and in the most important points of the naval base, using naval and military units of the P.A.O. [East Africa Police - 25 men];

d) The immediate recall from the decentralization location of a company of sailors of 120 men, to be kept on trucks available to the Command.

It was not possible to give instructions to the three Germanic minesweepers that were in port [in reality there were four: R 10, R 12, R 13, R 16] due to interruption of the connections, nor to contact the commander of the German base [Koruk 566], Major General Otto Deindl, to coordinate the actions, his command being 20 kilometers from Tobruk and the communication lines being interrupted. The alarm had already been given to the Germans at 10:45 pm on September 13th by Lieutenant Grelli of the DICAT Command, whose Anti-aircraft Group was responsible for the anti-aircraft defense of the square together with the Anti-aircraft Group of the Luftwaffe batteries (Flakgruppe Tobruk with the Flag-Regiment 114° and 914°), under the command of Colonel Hartmann.

---

34 AUSMM, "Relazione sull'attacco nemico alla Piazza di Tobruk nella notte sul 14 settembre 1942", Marilibia, cartella 15.

▲ Mid U.S. bombers B 25 of the 12th Group. On the night of September 14th they went to bomb the large airport of Quesada, where among other things Ju 87 of the three groups of St.G.3 were located. But the anti-aircraft succeeded in shooting down four aircrafts, since in the drop of the bombs they had constituted an excellent target, leaving the lights of the compartment of the bomb depot on.

▼ Italian anti-aircraft gun 75/46 mm from a sailors' station.

Lieutenant Grelli reported that enemy landing craft had been sighted. Subsequently, all two hundred men of the German anti-aircraft positions were put on alert to be ready to repel the attack. At the same time, without wasting time, with the usual efficiency the Germans moved their deadly 20mm machine gunnery complexes towards the port area, waiting for the events.

General Deindl, telephoning Tobruk, made it known to Captain Schultz-Ingenohol - chosen by him to command all German forces in the event of an attack on the port and fortress area - that he had assumed command of all German forces at Tobruk, and who would soon guide advanced forces along the Via Balbia to reach the destination. Having been informed at 00:20 on September 14th by Captain Schultz-Ingenohol that the enemy was landing 3 kilometers east of Tobruk, General Deindl ordered the pioneered motorized Batt. (Nachshub-Kol.Abt 909) to the 909th Batt. 715 men on staff: *"Landing of enemies in Tobruk. Move to cover the Gazala lines to via Balbia, the headquarters of 909 in Via Balbia at km 19 to be at my disposal"*. Then, at 00:30, General Deindl broadcast on the radio: *"Landing Alarm[35]"*.

Shortly afterwards, while he was gathering the forces of his two battalions (Pioneers 909° and 613° Morizzata Polizia Afrika Guards) at kilometer 19 of the Via Balbia to march on Tobruk, General Deindl informed Admiral Lombardi *"that he had hired in the night the Command of all the German forces of the Piazza"*, which at the command of Major Hardt included 1,440 men and men for the various services, to which were added 310 of the Luftwaffe commanded by Major Schewe for service at the airports[36].

This was his responsibility, since Admiral Lombardi was in charge of the command of the entire organization of the Navy and the naval vessels of Tobruk. But as we will see, when General Deindl arrived in the morning with his training groups, in time to participate in the raids, everything was practically finished, precisely because of the energetic initiative of Admiral Lombardi.

At 02:10 General Deindl informed Major Liehr, commander of the 613th Motorized Police Battalion Afrika Guards (with two companies the third was in Marsa Matruh), who was gathering his troops on Via Balbia, to move from kilometer 19, *"leaving behind small forces on the road to protect the coastal part north of the camps"*. He added that he was finding the means of transport with which to proceed quickly to Tobruk, moving along Via Balbia. So it was an aid to the defenders of the stronghold which was still very far away. In addition to these measures taken by General Otto Deindl, other ground forces were setting in motion to rush to the interior area of Tobruk, to make the British landing fail. It was not yet clear in which areas the enemy was landing, since the initial reports received by the command did not provide precise details, but it was believed that the British intended to try to *"take possession of the fortress"*. This threat was sufficient for Field Marshall Erwin Rommel (AOK) to bring together a force of German motorized troops for possible combat use in the event the British managed to occupy Tobruk. Consequently, the employment order concerned three units, which were:

1) The 580th Reconnaissance Battalion, who was ordered to move immediately to Marsa Matruh;
2) The 3rd reconnaissance Battalion which was to prepare pending notice of use;
3) The "Everth" battle group of the DAK (Deutsches Afrikakorps) which was to gather immediately a combat group, ready to go immediately to order, consisting of a battalion of Panzer Grenadier and a battalion of light artillery.

---

35 Peter C. Smith, *Massacre at Tobruk*, cit., pp. 136-137.
36 The numbers of the German forces, referring to the personnel and not to the availability of the moment, have been taken from Peter C. Smith's book, *Massacre at Tobruk*, which in many parts is very deficient and inaccurate, particularly on air attacks. The author's book was published in 1987 and at that time I had already printed for seven years *The German participation in the Mediterranean Sea War (1940-1945)*, afterwards all the Luftwaffe's attacks were reported for Tobruk's action, with a breakdown of the aircraft employed and their divisions. It was then followed in the newspaper "Il Giornale d'Italia" on January 6th and 7th, 1987 my article, even more complete with news, *The failed English landing in Tobruk on September 14th, 1942*, printed by "Il Giornale d'Italia" on January 7th, 1987..

While the alarm was raised in the stronghold, the men of Lieutenant Colonel Haselden, after having conquered battery no. 105 of the Italian Army, employed by the 2nd Anti-Aircraft Artillery Regiment, had been stopped by the staff of the nearby S.P. 5 (ex "Grasso") of the Regia Marina, located east of Marsa Beiad. The assailants, who entered the fence of the post, killed two soldiers on guard, and then seized the ammunition depot. But the men of the battery, entrenched behind the stands of the three 152 mm cannons, firing with individual weapons and throwing hand grenades, despite being largely injured, resisted by opposing for ten hours a tenacious resistance to the enemy, who then at first light of the day he had to surrender when, on trucks leaving at 02.20 from Tobruk, the command core of the San Marco Battalion led by the lieutenant of the ship arrived in the area of Marsa Sciausc. Giacomo Colotto[37].

This department of the Navy, *"with skillful and decisive action that lasted until the morning, countered the infiltration of the enemy, managing to surround him at dawn and to be right. The enemy losses in this episode were 8 dead, 10 seriously injured, 32 prisoners[38]"*. In the last phase of operations in Marsa Sciausc the San Marco department was reinforced with the company of 120 sailors organized to defend the Tobruk Command.

Among the British fallen, hit on the head on the beach around 03:30, there was also Lieutenant Colonel Haselden, to whom, found with the machine gun still clasped in his hands, he was given the honor of arms by the Italians.

Overall, in the areas of the landing points, apart from the British soldiers who managed to return with difficulty to the Sikh and Zulu destroyers and the torpedo boats, *"25 men were captured in the Marsa el Auda area, 40 in the Forte Perrone area and 30 in the area by Marsa Umm esc Sciausc. Another fifty prisoners were then captured during the mopping up operations[39]"*.

▲ Major General Otto Deindl and his officers. The picture is from May 1942.

---

37 A. Cocchia, *La difesa del tRAFfico con l'Africa Settentrionale. Dal 1° ottobre 1941 al 30 settembre 1942*, vol. VII, Roma, Ufficio Storico della Marina Militare, Roma, 1962, p. 350.
38 AUSMM, "Relazione sull'attacco nemico alla Piazza di Tobruk nella notte del 14 settembre 1942", Marilibia, cartella 15.
39 ASMEUS, "Comando Supremo, Sintesi delle operazioni svoltesi in Cirenaica (Tobruk) nella notte dal 13 al 14 settembre 1942"

▲ Men of San Marco Battalion in Tobruk.

Also at dawn, once the British command had been overwhelmed, the S.P. battery 5 was able to take part in the fire action against the enemy ships, firing his large 152 mm grenades from a great distance. As reported in the Diary of the Supreme Command[40]: *The land artillery, opened fire at the time of the air alarm, as soon as the landings started they acted first (11:40 pm) at the landing area of Marsa Umm Es Sciausc leaving the task of the anti-aircraft defense to the 88 Germanic batteries. In the second part of the night the artillery itself acted in two masses: one in the area north-west of Tobruk (Marsa El Auda-Forte Perrone-Marsa Abd El Crim) the other in the south-east area (Marsa Umm Esc Sciausc).*

According to the report of Admiral Lombardi (with all due respect to the Germans who believed they had done their own) the Batteries of the Royal Navy participated in the fire action: S.P. 5 (three 152/45 cannons), S.P. 3 (four 120/50 cannons), S.P. 21 (two cannons in twin 120/45 system), n. 19 (four 76/40 cannons); and the Milmart Batteries: 2nd (four 102/35 cannons), 6th (two 102/35 cannons), 25th (four 76/40 cannons); 29a (two 76/30 cannons), 27a (five 37/45 machine guns), 28a (five 20/65 machine guns). Apart from battery no. 105, which was the use of the various artillery of the 2nd anti-aircraft regiment, the first Italian unit that had engaged in combat against the landing of the Royal Marines in Marsa el-Auda.

Therefore, in the face of an unexpected fire reaction, the entire British frontal attack, however, carried out out of confidence, with absolutely insufficient forces, was destined to fail everywhere. And this thanks to the reaction of only the forces coordinated by Admiral Lombardi, including the German sailors of Tobruk, since the staff of the Flak remained in his defensive positions of the batteries, while the troops of General Deindl arrived, to a certain extent to be used in the action only after 05:30.

Therefore, it was specified in the report of the Italian Supreme Command[41]: *Our troops all behaved valiantly, resisting in place, intervening promptly, counterattacking. A lively spirit of collaboration, especially between the two Armed Forces - the Navy and the Army - to whom the honor and the burden of the struggle falls overnight. The maneuver of the few men and the artillery, rationally conducted, has allowed us to achieve maximum results. The command of the Interim Commander of the sector [Colonel Battaglia] and the coordination of the Command in the Piazza di Tobruk are excellent. [Admiral Lombardi] The action constitutes a brilliant Italian victory.*

▲ Italian soldiers defend a stretch of coast, armed with machine gun, rifle 91 and hand grenades.

---

40 SMEUS, Diario Storico del Comando Supremo, vol. e VIII, tomo II, Allegati, Roma, 1999, p. 63.
41 ASMEUS, "Comando Supremo, Sintesi delle operazioni svoltesi in Cirenaica (Tobruk) nella notte dal 13 al 14 settembre 1942".

▲ Breda heavy machine gun Mod. 37/54, air-cooled. Five of these anti-aircraft and land weapons were in the Milmart battery n. 27, and intervened in the Tobruk defense fights.

▼ Italian 105mm cannon of the Royal Army in Tobruk, for the defence of the fortress perimeter.

THE FAILURE OF BRITISH MOTOR TORPEDOES TO FORCE THE ENTRANCE TO THE PORT OF TOBRUK

At 01:45 on September 14th the six Force C torpedo-boats, with the commander, captain of vessel Denis Jermain on MTB 309, reached a distance of 2 miles by 270 degrees from Punta Tobruk. At 02:00 one of the units of the 15th Flotilla reported to MTB 309 that it had received the "Nigger" signal, transmitted by the signalers and indicating that Mersa Sciausc had been captured and the torpedo boats could approach to land the soldiers. Immediately Commander Jermain headed with his units to the southern coast of the Tobruk roadstead to look for the red signal lights, which were to be exposed there. but however much he and the other officers peered into the darkness, they saw nothing. Lieutenant Tommy B. Langton, the commander of SAS signalers, wrote in his report that the Aldis lamp to be used to give the torpedoes a go was unusable, and therefore he had to use a torch to transmit the three agreed red "Ts" signals every two minutes. Not seeing the signals, the commander Jermain then decided to do the thing deemed best: enter the port of Tobruk with the six torpedo boats to land the troops and see if there was any enemy ship to attack.

The first to approach were MTB 309, MTB 262 and MTB 266, but immediately, according to Commander Jermain, "the Germans" opened heavy crossfire on the three boats with light artillery and small caliber weapons fired from both sides of the inlet, and entrance to the harbor, and heavy and small caliber artillery from the north shore of the port. And he wrote in his report: *"It was obvious to me, due to the heavy opposition, that Mersa Sciausc had not been captured by British troops, or that those troops had been rejected[42]"*.

That first attempt by British torpedo boats to land troops, which occurred after Force B had signaled that the road was clear, failed mainly due to the prompt reaction of the Italian motor raft MZ 733 (second lieutenant of Calderara vessel), located with the MZ 759 (lieutenant Fulvi) in reinforcement near the obstructions at the entrance to the harbor, while a third motor raft, the MZ 756, had been decentralized in Marsa el Baiad a few hours ago. At 01:00 the MZ 733 sent to the Marina Tobruk Command: *"Enemy torpedo boats tried to force the obstructions. I am going to attack"*; in this clash between motor rafts and torpedo boats, the sailors of the MZ 733, entrenched behind sandbags, began to shoot with submachine guns and muskets and when the cannon 76 at the stern had run out of ammunition, continued to shoot against the opposing hulls, keeping them away, using lighting projectiles.

Only the two torpedoes MTB 314 (Lieutenant of vessel Harwin Woodthorpe Sheldrick) and MTB 261 (Lieutenant of vessel C.C. Anderson), acting independently, managed to enter an inlet and unload a section of riflemen of the Royal Northumberland Regiment. MTB 314, with the ship's lieutenant on board. C.P. Everson, perhaps having been hit by the shot of the MZ 733 and poorly steering, ran aground on the rocky coast and it was not possible to free it. In the meantime, Lieutenant Langton, leaving the signal torch lit in a rock, had gone to the disembarkation point and found MTB 314 and MBT 261 that straano unloading the men and the material. Then he went back to where he had left the flashlight, and shortly thereafter he saw the strong light of a spotlight that lit up on the opposite bank of the port towards the sea and then went to illuminate a torpedo-torpedoes and moving his beam go to look for others. It was the group of torpedo boats of the frigate captain Robert Alexander Allen, commander of the 10th Flotilla, who had arrived in front of Tobruk shortly after the six hulls of the captain of vessel Jermain. The enemy's spotlights were crossing the water like red lines and, in a fantastic scenario, the beams of the projectors moved across the sea, trying to locate a target for their artillery. Commander Allan was unable to find a passage in defense of the barrier, and therefore three

---

42 Dudley B.E. Pope, *Flag 4-The Battle of Coastal Forces in the Mediterranean 1939-1945*, London, Chatham Publishing, 1954, p. 60.

of his MTBs launched torpedos towards the barrier to try to detonate a part of it to open a passage. But the British were unfortunate, because every time they tried to get closer to find out something, the beams of light from the harbor spotlights directed towards them. According to the report of Admiral Lombardi, of motor rafts, armed with a 76 mm cannon and a 20 mm machine gun, in Tobruk there were twenty-two of the Regia Marina (of the German type MFP, built in Italian shipyards), to which they had to add other sects on the German side [F 343, F 349, F 352, F 358, F 359, F 360 and F 362]; but only towards dawn they were placed in a suitable position to contribute to the defense of the base and the port, which is why in the hottest moment of the first enemy action only the three aforementioned motor-rafts MZ 733, MZ 756 and MZ 759 could engage successfully. Even the second attempt by the Force C torpedo bombers to force the blockade to land troops in Marsa Sciausc, failed around 03:30 on September 14th. Arriving at slow motion below the coast to evade exploration, the torpedo boats were unable to pass due to the energetic reaction exerted by the MZ 756 motor-raft (Longo vessel second lieutenant), who sighted the enemy and reacted with his weapons, the 76 mm cannon and the 20mm machine gun. Immediately afterwards the cannons from Italian torpedo boats Castore (three pieces of 100 mm), General Carlo Montanari and General Antonino Cascino (six pieces of 102 mm each[43]), and the two 120 mm cannons of the Dandolo battery opened fire.

But in particular, the British crews were impressed by the shooting of the German 20mm squared machine guns of the 3rd battery of the 914th Regiment (3./914) of the Tobruk Contraereo Group, which, having promptly moved from its normal position in the port area, developed a heavy fire on the torpedo boats that tried to approach the entrance of the bay of Mersa es Sciausc. To their shooting was added that of the 20 mm quadruple machine-guns of the battery 4./914 of Captain Frintrop, and all this contributed to the decision of the thin-hull motor torpedoes to withdraw.

Nobody, apparently, noticed the torpedoes launched on targets glimpsed in the bay by the three torpedo boats that were lost without making the defensive barrier of the port or the ships that were found there no damage. On the Italian side, it was believed that one of the British torpedoes hit by projectiles was moving away with fire on board and a long trail of smoke.

Commander Jermain withdrew to the east in consideration of the large volume of small arms fire that the enemy fired against his units, which were scattered. He brought together three and at 05:45 he made a further attempt to enter Marsa Sciausc, but once again he met a deadly barrage with heavy and light weapons. Then Commander Jermain retired again, planning to try a new attempt at dawn; but shortly after sunrise with the start of the airstrikes, by order received, he had to report to the four torpedo boats who were with him and to two motolances who were close, to resume the route to return to Alexandria.

---

[43] Each torpedo boat was armed with three cannons, the 100mm Castore, the Cascino and the 102mm Montanari. In addition, each torpedo boat had four 20 mm twin machine gunner complexes.

▲ A Regia Marina motorboat is proceeding along the rocky and steep Libyan coast. They were armed with a 76mm cannon and a single 20mm machine gun located aft. In a later version, a second 20mm machine gun was added to the hull.

▼ The torpedo boat Castore of the "Spica" class in a Libyan port protected by the fence of the torpedo nets.

▲ The old torpedo boat Antonino Cascino.

▼ 20 mm Flakvierling 38 quadruple machine gunner.

THE SINKING OF THE DESTROYER SIKH

In the meantime that the landing of Force C troops was not successful, but rather turned into a disaster for the attackers, there was a big loss for Force A. Shortly before 01:00 on September 14th the Sikh and Zulu destroyers had reached positions assigned to them off Marsa el Mreisa, starting the landing of the first contingent of the 350 soldiers they carried[44].

But the Carley dinghies, put into the sea, which was somewhat choppy, after having brought ashore a first core of 70 Royal Marines, did not go back. And this was due to an error by the submarine of the 1st Taku Flotilla (captain of corvette Jack Gethin Hopkins) who, leaving Porto Said on September 9th, mistakenly recognizing the coast, landed the beacon in Marsa el Adua; that is, in a point located 5 km further west of Marsa el Mreisa, where the signals with red lights coming from the ground (02:45 am) directed the boats with the troops[45].

▲ A twin complex of 120mm cannons in the shielded turret of the Zulu destroyer. Servants load the pieces.

---

44 Dudley B.E. Pope, *Flag 4-The Battle of Coastal Forces in the Mediterranean 1939-1945*, London, Chatham Publishing, 1954, p. 60.
45 The presence of Taku off Tobruk was reported to the local Marine Command at sunset on September 13th, and after that a convoy composed by the steamer Sibilla escorted by the torpedo boat Montanari, sailed from the port a short time before, had been ordered to return immediately. The search for the submarine by all available vessels in Tobruk remained unsuccessful.. Cfr. AUSMM, Marilibia, b. 15, "Relazione sull'attacco nemico alla Piazza di Tobruk nella notte sul 14 settembre 1942".

Major R.P. Livingstone described the dramatic landing episode as follows[46]: *The sea was far from calm, the destroyers rolled and the barges that had to be towed by two motorboats, they could barely float, but somehow the men of the first team managed to descend, and at 3:48 the two rows of clumsy boats headed uncertainly into the darkness towards the only dim light that could be seen ashore. Half an hour later, a radio signal arrived from Colonel Unwin. His engine had failed and he and the boats he towed were drifting, unable to reach the shore or return to the ships. So that of the marine riflemen, half were still on board the destroyers, a quarter went adrift and the remaining quarter was, perhaps on the ground, but without devices to communicate, because that of Colonel Unwin was the only radio. At 05:00 on the beach began to fight; the destroyers drew even closer to land, and the Sikh found some of the barges drifting. As he was gathering the men, some spotlights lit up in the sky, swayed, and then pinned themselves full on the destroyer. From a short distance the coastal batteries opened fire, aiming directly, and they were joined by the 88 anti-aircraft guns.*

As a result, although the Sikh and the Zulu had landed in Marsa el Mreisa a company of two Royal Marines platoons under the command of Major Jack Hedley, following the disservice of the signalers of the submarine Taku the landing, already opposed on the beach by the gunners Italians of the 2nd anti-aircraft regiment lined up in the area, who opened fire on enemy landing craft, illuminated at a distance of 700 m with spotlights with machine guns, and mortars, ended up ending with the capture of all British soldiers; and this also happened due to the arrival of the mixed mobile defense company, comprising forty sailors, forty Royal Carabinieri of the 18th Battalion, and a platoon of thirty German sailors from the Tobruk Maritime Transport Office commanded by corvette captain Paul Meixner, Head of the Landings Office with North Africa (Seetransportchef für Nordafrika). To these one hundred and ten men, hastily collected in Tobruk and sent to face the threat looming north of the base, were added, during the transfer march, another fifty carabinieri with the commander of the 18th battalion[47].

Major Hadley with 21 other marines, the only survivors of his two platoons who had remained hidden in a wadi, surrendered in the morning during the raking of Italian troops. In a report of the Supreme Command it is written[48]: *Our forces on the ground - having managed to contain the enemy everywhere - were definitely on the counterattack. Later German training groups joined in reinforcement in the meantime. The actions, at the various landing points, ended by throwing the opponent back everywhere, capturing 25 prisoners in the Marsa Auda area, 40 in the Forte Perrone area and 30 in the Marsa Umm esc Sciausc area. Another fifty prisoners were then captured during the mopping up operations. In total, 58 British dead were counted ashore, regardless of those who fell overboard or drowned when their awkward and unmanageable landing boats were slammed against the rocks, and 650 prisoners were captured, including over 30 officers, mostly recovered at sea.*

Of the men engaged on the ground against the Tobruk stronghold, only ten managed to undertake the long march to reach El Alamein, but only six of them, with Lieutenant David Lanark (real name David Russell) were able to return to the British lines, which reached the November 18th after a very long march, surviving only for the help received by the Arabs. Overall, according to the data reported in the Historical Diary of the Supreme Command on the basis of a report received by the Command of Field Marshal Rommel, the losses of the Axis forces reported to Tobruk on the day of September 14th were represented by "*54 dead and 29 wounded between staff of the Royal Navy and "S.Marco" battalion, 16 dead (1 German) and about 50 injured (7 Germans) among the ground departments[49]*".

---

46 R.P. Livingstone, "Le grandi incursioni nel deserto", *Storia della seconda guerra mondiale*, cit., p. 3.
47 For the defense of the Tobruk stronghold there were the 3rd Battalion San Marco of the Navy with 460 men, about 100 Carabinieri of the 18th Battalion, elements of the 5th Libyan Battalion, a Navy formation company, and servants of the numerous coastal positions, twelve of which anti-aircraft, the latter represented, as said, by six batteries of German 88 and 20 mm guns, and six batteries of various Italian guns of the 1st Group of the MILMART (Maritime Artillery Militia). During the day they also served two battalions with about 700 German soldiers, but before nightfall they moved to a base several kilometers from Tobruk. At their posts remained the servants of the anti-aircraft and coastal batteries, and the men engaged at checkpoints along the access road to Tobruk..
48 ASMEUS, "Comando Supremo, Sintesi delle operazioni svoltesi in Cirenaica (Tobruk) nella notte dal 13 al 14 settembre 1942".
49 SMEUS, Diario Storico del Comando Supremo, vol. e VIII, tomo II, Allegati, Roma, 1999, p. 140.

▲ The British submarine Taku, which carried marine landing beacons from Force A destroyers on the northern part of the Tobruk Peninsula.

▼ From the left, Captain St. John Aldrich Micklethwait, commander of the Sikh and 22nd Destroyer Flotilla of the Mediterranean Fleet, and Lieutenant Colonel E.H.M. Urwin, Commander of the 11th Battalion. Royal Marines.

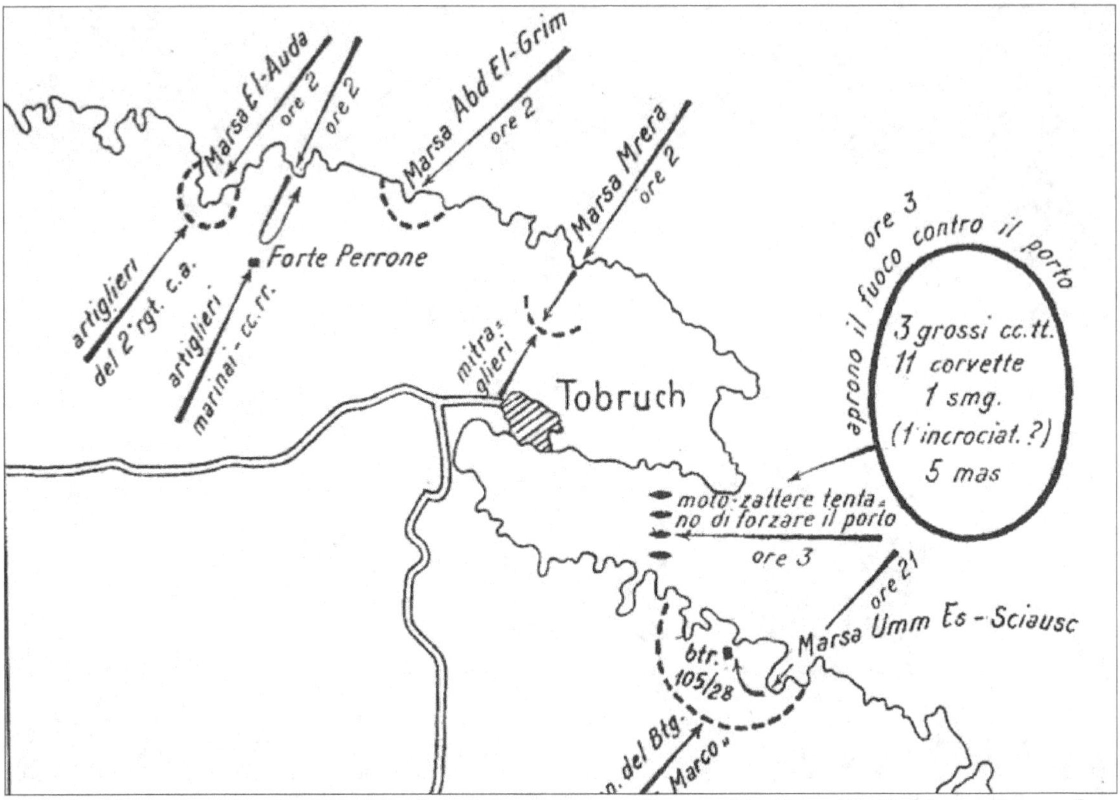

▲ The British attack on Tobruk on the night of 13-14th September 1942. Charter of the General Staff of the Royal Army, from the Historical Diary of the Supreme Command.

▼ Marine from Force A, rescued by a destroyer, sleeping exhausted on deck.

According to other subsequent sources, the Italo-German casualties were 62 in total and 119 injured. While the British attack was underway, on the Italian side numerous reinforcements were sent to Tobruk, with rotated vehicles leaving from Derna, Bir el Gazala, Bi Amu and Bardia. They included four troop battalions, two artillery batteries, an armored personnel carrier, a regiment command, which however following reports from Tobruk indicating that the enemy action had failed, it was not necessary to take action. On the German side, the motorized departments that were marching from Marsa Matruh or who were ready to receive the order of departure from the front line of El Alamein, fearing that the British could take possession of the square of Tobruk, were recalled when the Command of Field Marshal Rommel realized that the forces that were in the stronghold had managed on their own *"to restore the situation[50]"*.

At 05:26 on September 14th, the Commander in Chief of the Mediterranean, Admiral Harwood, informed the British Admiralty that the landing of Force A had failed and that the Sikh destroyer had been hit and immobilized, and at 06:23 he added that the commander of Force C in the Tobruk area had reported what the situation was and that he had to order the remaining torpedo boats to retire. According to Italian reports, during the troubled landing operations of British troops, the Sikh and Zulu destroyers had opened fire at 04:00 from the distance of 6,000 m, targeting coastal batteries and naval targets in the port[51]. The batteries, illuminating the two naval units with the spotlights, responded promptly, even from a short distance, with direct aiming shooting, also making use of illuminating projectiles. The batteries of the Navy "Belotti" with four 145 mm cannons, "S.P. 3" (ex "Thrush") with four 120 mm cannons, and" S.P. 21" (formerly "Dandolo"), with a 120 mm twin assembly, and subsequently, towards the end of the action, around 05:00, also the "S.P. 5" (ex "Fat"), freed from the pressure of the commandos that attacked her, firing with her three 152 mm pieces[52]. Validly backed by the six Germanic 88 mm guns of the 76th Battery (Lieutenant Müller-Frank) of the 1st Department of the 46th Germanic Anti-aircraft Regiment (Flak-Abt. I./46), under the authority of Major Wilhelm Wegener and located in Punta Tobruk, the artillery of the Royal Navy fired uninterruptedly on the two British destroyers until day gone, with excellent results.

Also intervening against the planes, the Navy batteries alone fired 2,316 projectiles, of which 37 from 152 mm, 668 from 120, 689 from 102, 922 from 76, 169 from 37 mm. We can see from Admiral Lombardi's report how the fire action of the batteries developed against the two British destroyers: *At about 04:00 they were spotted about 6000 meters from the coast, first one and then two more, silhouettes of enemy ships, which were initially believed to be cruisers while they were in effect large destroyers. Shortly afterwards the two enemy units opened fire on the coastal batteries, which promptly responded by making use of illuminants. The fire action lasts uninterrupted until the day is done. Many salvos fell in the northern area of Tobruk around the coastal batteries; others in the port and on the southern ridge. The blanks, which sometimes appeared to be 152 mm caliber, sometimes 120 mm caliber, were fairly compact and at least four strokes each. From the naval bombing action only the SIBILLA steamship was hit, by two shots of 100, on the left side of the dead work; one of the shots exploded with slight damage the other did not explode. The medium-caliber and anti-aircraft batteries deployed in the north area took part in the shooting against the enemy; and towards the end of the action also the ex GRASSO battery (R. Marina S.P. 5) freed, with the help of the San Marco battalion, from the assailants. The ex DANDOLO 120 battery (R. Marina S.P. 21), although still being assembled, came into action with a twin piece armed by R. Marina personnel in charge of the work.*

At the first light of dawn, enemy units are recognized for SIKH type destroyers. Around 04:55 following a medium-caliber salvo [and therefore not 88 mm pieces], a fire broke out on an enemy destroyer [SIKH]. The unit covered itself with curtains of fog extended also by another destroyer [ZULU], and slowly moved away towards the northeast.

50 ASMEUS, "Comando Supremo, Sintesi delle operazioni svoltesi in Cirenaica (Tobruk) nella notte dal 13 al 14 settembre 1942"; Erwin Rommel, *Krieg ohne hass*, Milano, Garzanti, 1952, p. 229.
51 National Archives, ADM 223/565.
52 AUSMM, "Comando Marina Tobruk, Attacco nemico alla Piazza di Tobruk", Marilibia, cartella 15.

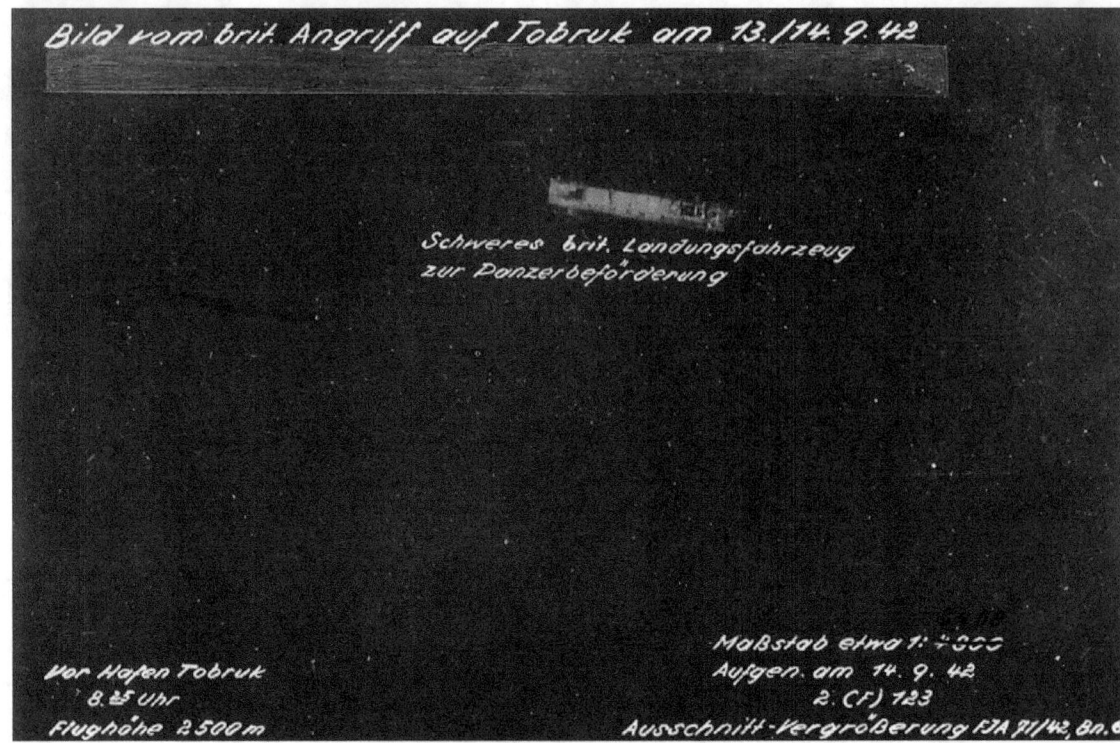

▲ The image, taken at 08:25 a.m. on September 14th from a Ju 88 D reconnaissance vehicle from the 2.(F)/123 of the X Fliegerkorps shows, according to the caption, a sinking landing craft. From the shape it seems instead to be a Axis raft. According to the German Navy's War Log of September 13th, a German raft went aground in shallow waters after a mine exploded.

▼ The modest British landing craft used in tow abandoned along the northern coast of the Tobruk peninsula and captured by the Germans.

▲ MILMART's 152/50 mm coastal cannon battery, similar to those that defended the Tobruk stronghold in the S.P.5 (ex Grasso) battery. On the top right a large projector to illuminate at night enemy ships and planes sighted at sea.

▼ The same battery is about to receive the signal to open fire.

Around 05:00 another enemy unit was hit in the stern by a salvo and remained immobilized...The VEGA tugboat was sent to attempt the towing of one of the two affected destroyers (later identified as SIKH) which however sank at 07:52. Shortly after the sinking of the SIKH the other destroyer blew up with a strong explosion (later identified as the ZULU) who had left with a fire on board.

Also from the Supermarina Report "Damage inflicted on the Enemy", it appears that *"around 04:00 two enemy destroyers [later ascertained for Sikh and Zulu] opened the drone against the ground, but were promptly countered by our anti-ship batteries [Thrush and Dandolo]. At 04:20 a [Sikh] destroyer was hit by a salvo and a fire was seen to develop in the bow: the unit moved away to the north-east covered by fog spread by the other destroyer. At 06:30 this was also hit [was always the Sikh] by a stern in the stern and was immobilized. Around 0600 three motor torpedo boats were also hit by the shooting of the batteries... At 07:52 the destroyer immobilized at 06:30 sank near Tobruk.*

Finally, according to an in-depth report by Supermarina (see Annex 1), at 05:05 a destroyer was framed by a medium-sized salvo, and a forward fire was seen to develop. The unit was covered by a curtain of smoke spread by another destroyer, and slowly moved away to the northeast. Then, around 05:55, one of the two enemy units was hit by a salvo at the stern and was immobilized[53].

This presentation of the facts, with precise times, then serves to make a comparison on what the hits were really hit, and which did the most damage, by the Italian batteries on the two British destroyers.

▲ A 75mm Italian anti-aircraft gun.

---

53 AUSMM, "Relazione sull'attacco nemico alla Piazza di Tobruk nella notte sul 14 settembre 1942", Marilibia, cartella 15.

The first destroyer to be targeted was the Sikh, commanded by vessel captain St. John Aldrich Micklethwait, who had headed for the coast to search for boats that had not returned after the landing of the first troops. While the Sikh gathered the soldiers on their boats at 05:05 am [around 04:00 am for the Italians] suddenly a lighthouse came on on the coast. The Zulu moved quickly away, while the Sikh instead found himself on the spotlight beam, and immediately the Italian coastal batteries Tordo and Dandolo opened fire with 152 and 102 mm guns. A medium-caliber bullet, which exploded on the Sikh in the wheelhouse area, damaged the lubrication and rudder feeding system and immobilized it. A second forward shot blew up the ammunition depot of the cannons of the binate tower A giving rise to a violent fire that killed, wounded or burned in the bridge the Royal Marines who had just been recovered from their small boats and trapped others in the lower bridges.

At this point the cannons of the forward towers A and B responded to the fire aiming at the spotlights but with little effect. In the meantime the German Flak battery (I / 43) with 88 mm cannons had come into action. Due to the failure of the rudder, the Sikh circulated at a speed of 10 knots, which however tended to decrease. A third bullet hit the direction of the rangefinder and from then on all the destroyer guns had to fire under visual control. While the Sikh, at 05:20, stopped in flames, unable, even for the damage to the rudder, to make any movement, Captain Micklethwait stopped the cars and ordered the Zulu to take his destroyer in tow. So, having found that other spotlights had sighted some torpedo boats to the east and that they too were under fire, believing that the game was lost and it was time to save further losses and save the salvable, he ordered all British naval forces to get away.

▲ A German 88mm cannon is placed in a coastal defense position. In Tobruk it equipped the 76th battery of the 46th Anti-aircraft Regiment (Flak) intervened, from Tobruk point against British ships together with four Italian batteries with 102, 120, 152 mm cannons.

▲ In dry land, the 2 L. FIt boat, captured by German sailors who hoisted their flag there.

▼ The same taken to the sea near the coast of the port of Tobruk.

The Zulu destroyer, commanded by frigate captain Richard Taylor White, who was also struck and damaged by the rain of bullets fired from the coastal batteries, took the Sikh in tow, at 05:30, attempted to drag him offshore.

But during the towing, a bullet hit the Zulu on the formwork causing him to release the towing cable with the Sikh, who was hit again by a fourth bullet, originating the development of a strong fire in the stern. A fifth bullet hit tower B in the bow killing the servants of the cannons. Other men took their places and the two cannons kept firing. In the meantime, the Zulu tried to retake the Sikh's trailer, but he was hit by a sixth bullet on the bridge, which increased the intensity of the fires. By now it was dawn and the two British destroyers, visible to the fire of the enemy artillery (of the Italian batteries Tordo, Dandolo, and Grasso and of the German I / 76) fixed the trailer, were about to begin to move to move away from the coast when another bullet it hit the area of the towing cable of the Sikh who again broke away.

There was no hope of saving the much damaged destroyer. The Zulu laid a curtain of smoke around the Sikh and again approached it with the intention of taking the crew aboard. But the maneuver, under a shower of bullets, was too dangerous, and Captain Micklethwait wisely ordered the Zulu - who had been hit by two bullets suffering various structural damage and light flooding in four compartments - to move away to save himself. The bullets from the Italian and German cannons continued to hit the Sikh, who could only fire back with the aft tower X until the bullets from his depot ran out, and there was no possibility of bringing more. Then, Captain Micklethwait, after giving the order to abandon ship, activated the sinking charges which exploded and flooded the engine and boiler rooms. Then he made one last turn of his ship and then lowered himself into the sea with the survivors.

▲ The British Sikh destroyer arriving in Malta, in the Grand Harbor, in January 1942, escorting a convoy that left Alexandria.

▲ The wonderful 88 mm cannon of the Flak in its mobile carriage.

▼ On the left, the captain of vessel Richard Taylor Whit commander of the destroyer ZULU. Right, Lt. Vessel George Raymond Worledge commander of the ML 352 motorboat.

Meanwhile, at 05:26 the Commander of the 22nd Flotilla, on the Sikh, I signal to the Command of the Mediterranean Fleet that the landing of the troops of Force A had failed and that his destroyer had been hit and immobilized, but that he was trying to get him back on the move. Then at 06:04 he added *"My 0526 Zulu is trying to take me in tow"*. And at 06:23 the news arrived in Alexandria that Force A was withdrawing and that the commander of Force C in the Tobruk area, reporting that the situation was critical, asked for orders for the torpedo boats, evidently to gather troops or to withdraw.

Major Livingstone wrote: *"It was evident that the game was lost, and it was time to try to save further losses and save the salvable[54]"*.

As we will see, the Sikh, not yet sunk, had been attacked by some Italian fighter-bombers Mc 200 of the 13th Group of the 2nd Fighter Wing, who hit him on the bridge with a modest 50-pound bomb, and at the same time, even if abandoned by the constituting an excellent target, highly visible in daylight, it had been reached by other artillery shells. Then, at 06:30 the Sikh was cannonized by escort destroyer Croome (corvette captain Rupert Cyril Egan), who had been sent to the area, together with his twin Hursley (vessel lieutenant William John Patrick Church), by the commander of Force D, on the Coventry anti-cruiser. The Croone gave the Sikh the coup de grace after recovering part of the crew. The Sikh sank, exploding, in a lat. 32°05'N, long. 24° 00'E, while part of the survivors, reached the nearby coast, they were taken prisoner and ended up in a concentration camp in Italy. Vessel captain Micklethwait was recovered two hours after having descended into the sea with his other men from Italian rescue vessels. Between the crew and the Sikh soldiers there were one hundred and fifteen dead.

▲ The Sikh destroyer's 40mm pom-pom quadrate anti-aircraft complex reacting to an airstrike.

---

54 R.P. Livingstone, "Le grandi incursioni nel deserto", *Storia della seconda guerra mondiale*, cit., p. 311.

There are still discussions on who to credit the sinking of the Sikh by consulting the Internet Forums. It is sure, from our reconstruction and from the map of the Supermarina report (see below) that the first shots were received by the Italian batteries Dandalo, Tordi and Belotti, and that I was then finished by the concentrated shot of the batteries Dandolo, Tordo, 76 (I ./43) and Grasso. So we can consider it an indisputable success, at least halfway through the second phase of the fight, between Italians and Germans. But at this point, as if by magic, it appears from the book by Peter C. Smith, Massacre at Tobruk of 1976, that according to the German combat report, the vital blows that had immobilized and then finished the Sikh, would not have been caused by the shot of the 88 mm I./43 battery of Major Weneger, which is not even mentioned, but to another German Flak battery, also with 88 mm cannons, the I / 60 of Captain Nitziki. Which, like Peter C. Smith, makes us perplexed also because the location of that anti-aircraft battery, certainly not located near the northern ridge of Tobruk, and therefore much further away from the British destroyers, we ignore it. It should also be considered that the cannons of the anti-aircraft batteries, engaged for hours to counter the bombing of enemy planes, being in their positions in a fixed position, to be strictly respected, were certainly not moved to bring them closer to the coast. Therefore, for the anti-ship intervention of the I / 60 it is possible that it was a transcription error in the combat report. The Zulu, after receiving the command of the 22nd Flotilla to move away from his condemned Sikh to reach the "Hunt" escort destroyers of the 5th Flotilla, in retreating east, initially at the speed of 30 knots, joined the Hursley and at Croome.

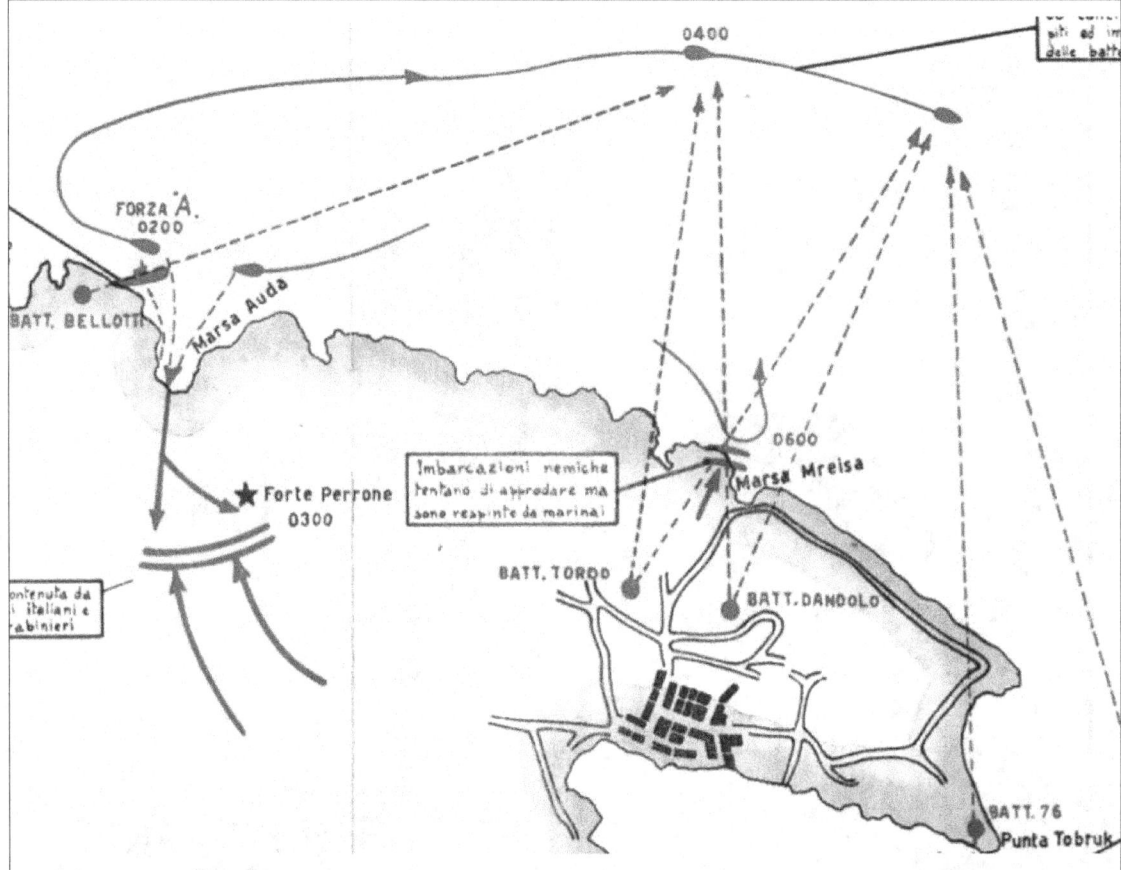

▲ The fire action of the batteries of the Tobruk coastal defense against the British Sikh and Zulu destroyers. From left the Bellotti, Tordo, Dandolo, 76 batteries (German I / 43 Flak) and the last dash is the shot of the S.P.5 battery (Grasso), more backward. The German presumption, accepted by the British, that the battery 76 (I / 43), the furthest on the map from the Sikh and the one with the least powerful bullets, intervening at a later time sank, alone, the destroyer is a pretext and cannot be accepted. USMM map reduction.

Then, he reached the cruiser Coventry who, before reversing the route to Alexandria, by order received at 09:00 had moved to Tobruk to also give protection to the ships that were withdrawing north-east in detached groups, leaving the it costs at the maximum speed allowed for the various types of vehicles. To chase the retreating British naval units and to rake the sea area in front of the port of Tobruk, Admiral Lombardi brought out the torpedo boats Castore and Montanari from the port, but they were unable to make contact with the enemy ships that were rapidly moving away, hammered by the Italian and German aviation. Then, *"In relation to the presence of shipwrecks and stopped and damaged units at sea"*, Marina Tobruk brought out three German minesweeper motorcycles of the 6th Flotilla and five motor-rafts, four German and one Italian, out of twenty-two available, all armed with cannon and machine gun[55]. On that day September 14th it appeared that the 6th minesweeper squadron of corvette captain Peter Reischauer had twenty-two units available in various ports of Libya and Italy and that four of them were in Tobruk: R 10, R 12, R 13 and R 16.

The recovery of the Sikh was not possible by the Italian tugboat Vega, brought out specifically from the port by order of Command Marina Tobruk, protected by the two torpedo boats because, as he approached, the immobilized destroyer in flames was seen to explode violently and sink at 07:52. With the now cleared bay of the surviving British thin units, the Axis naval vessels remained to devote themselves to rescue at sea, collecting and *"bringing ashore, 468 shipwrecks, mostly navies, with 23 officers including a captain of vessel [the commander of the Sikh] and an American journalist"*.

▲ German minesweeper of the 6th bataillon on the Libic coast

55 ASMEUS, "Comando Supremo, Sintesi delle operazioni svoltesi in Cirenaica (Tobruk) nella notte dal 13 al 14 settembre 1942".

The German minesweeper of the 6th Flotilla collected 117 shipwrecked, but it is not clear if their number results in that of the 458 shipwrecked in the Italian report.

In addition, the German R 10 minesweeper, commanded by the lieutenant Peter Reischeauer, commander of the 6th Flotilla, was lucky to find the MTB 314 torpedo-torpedo (former US PT 56) which, as we have said, in forcing the entry of the port of Tobruk had run aground in Marsa Sciausc. The small British unit, commanded by Lt. Vessel Harwin Woodthorpe Sheldrick, had been abandoned by the men of his crew, who, before being collected by MTB 261 of Lt. Vessel Charles Courtney Anderson, had unsuccessfully attempted to destroy their ship with an explosive charge that hadn't activated. Approaching the immobilized MTB 314, the R 10 minesweeper captured it practically unscathed and, after unhinging it, drove it to port with the German flag on the shore. It must be said that the British, through their cryptographic organization Ultra, immediately became aware of the capture of MTB 314, and this regard the curiosity of the readers can be contained in the chapter which describes the decryptions of the Ultra, transmitted to the Author, together with other important documents of the "Agreement" operation by his friend Platon Alexiades, a famous Canadian historian of Greek origin. It must be said that the Germans asked Supermarina to be able to keep possession of the torpedo-boat, to replace one of their lost minesweeper motorcycles. In response, with a letter dated October 1st 1942 for the Command of the German Navy in Italy, Admiral Arturo Riccardi reported that although for the rules of international law, and for the provisions issued by the Supreme Command before the offensive in Egypt, the Navy Italian had "the right" to take possession of the MTB 314 torpedo-boat, *"to offer a joint certificate of recognition to the value of the Allied Navy"*, renounced that right. However, he asked *"to allow Italian technicians to visit it thoroughly"*, to examine its *"technical systems"*. This was allowed as our following photographs demonstrate[56]. Renamed RA 10 and put into service in the German Navy as a torpedo transport unit, the torpedo torch was sunk on April 30th 1943 at Augusta (Sicily) in the attack of four Spitfire fighter aircraft of the 249th RAF Squadron, which took off from Malta. According to another source it was sunk, always under the same date and by bombings of RAF planes, on the northern coasts of Tunisia, near La Goulette.

▲ The MZ 715 sailing along the North African coast. After the retreat of the surviving British units, the motor rafts dedicated themselves to the hipwreckeds' collection.

---

56 AUSMM, *Scontri navali e operazioni di guerra*, cartella 91.

▲ The British MTB 314 torpedo boat after being captured in Tobruk by the German minesweeper R 10.

▼ The same British torpedo MTB 314.

▲ The dashboard of the MTB 314 torpedo torch and an officer of the Italian Navy, upon request authorized to view the characteristics of the unit.

▼ One of the two torpedo launchers of the MTB 314 torpedo torch, which had four in total.

THE AXIS AIR FORCE'S ATTACKS

Starting from the dawn of September 14th, the Italian and German aviation also intervened in the battle with all the available means against British naval vessels in the Tobruk area, and in the initial actions the Mc 200 aircraft of the 13th Hunting Group of the 5th were particularly distinguished Aerial of Libya, commanded by Major Lorenzo Viale.

This superior officer, acting on his own initiative due to the interruption of connections with the Eastern Sector Command of the 5th Air Team, *"after an offensive reconnaissance to realize the situation and act accordingly"*, carried out on the enemy naval units in retreat twenty one missions with Mc 200 aircraft, ordering pilots to attack with bombs and the strafing of the main enemy units that he had identified to the north-west of Tobruk, and with a secondary objective the strafing of the torpedoes that were located east-north-east of the port.

The aircraft, taking off from the base of Bu Amud, east of Tobruk, between 05:55 and 08:00 attacked diving from an altitude of 2,500 m, descending, to drop the bombs between 1,000 and 500 m in height, for then at low altitude, in sections of two - three Mc 200 at a time, carry out strafing. For the first time, the 13th Group aircraft used 50 kg bombs, which were once required to carry out exercises.

During his reconnaissance, Major Viale had made the following sightings[57]: *A group of ships made up of 9 unspecified units crossing 60 kilometers north of Tobruk, a group made up of 1 cruiser or large C.T. plus 3 C.T. 2 km north Marsa El Auda heading north, a group consisting of 2 torpedo boats or large patrol boats plus 9 torpedo boats in the north sea area Marsa Es Zeitun heading North East.*

Major Viale, which had only nine efficient Mc 200s in Bu Amud, wrote: *"A few days ago I had been instructed to train my pilots in the dive bombing. As soon as the bombs arrived I decided to practice on a wreck of an English steamer right in front of us but fate decided otherwise".*

The mounting of the bombs on the wings of the Mc 200s, who were at their first action in that new attack on the sea specialty, proved somewhat difficult due to the scarcity of personnel, and because it was necessary to unload the additional tanks.

At the same time Viale also managed[58]: *... to continuously ensure the protection of the port of Tobruk with cruises and at the same time in addition to the alarm patrol on Macchi 202 [two aircraft] keep a section of Macchi 200 ready to intervene, if necessary, to reinforce the alarm patrol itself.*

Each time the planes returned, the pilots provided news of the ships hit and sunk, and this generated moments of unbridled enthusiasm and joy among the staff of the group and the airport.

But, let's see what the results were really achieved in the course of the attacks, starting from the moment in which the Mc 200s of the greater Viale, of the 78th, 79th and 82nd squadrons who, dropping the 50 kg bombs and firing 12.7 explosive bullets mm, they first hit with a bomb, disintegrating, the motor torpedo torpedo MTB 312 (vessel lieutenant. Jan A. Quarrie), whose survivors, crew and soldiers, were collected by MTB 266 (second lieutenant of vessel John Norman Broad).

Various motor torpedoes were then machine-gunned and damaged by the Mc 200s, and the two motor-boats ML 353 (lieutenant of vessel. ES Michelson), and ML 352 (lieutenant of vessel. George Raymond Worledge), sunk one after the other, which having a speed of only 18 knots and carrying a load of demolition and particularly flammable liquids on the deck, such as petrol from the engines, once hit exploded after igniting.

The ML 353, after being abandoned by the crew collected by the ML 349 (captain of corvette AH Ball), was burning at the surface of the sea, but to ensure that it was not towed by the enemy, when the last men had abandoned it they were made shine the demolition charges.

---

57 Archivio Stato Maggiore Aeronautica Ufficio Storico (d'ora in poi ASMAUS), "Relazione attività 13° Gruppo C.T.".
58 *Ibidem*

The ML 352 crew was collected by the Italian torpedo boat Castore, commanded by the lieutenant Gaspare Tezel and brought to Tobruk as a prisoner of war[59].

▲ British motolance sailing.

---

[59] On the loss of ML 352 we have the following report of its commander, Lieutenant Worledge, who was outside the port of Tobruk to implement the disembarkation of the spoilers. He was ordered to wait while ML349 left to check the situation. When the ML349 did not return to report, Commander Worledge headed for the Tobruk harbor and at one point was confronted with what he thought was the silhouette of an Italian destroyer, when in fact it was supposed to be one of three torpedo boats, if not one of the rafts at the entrance to the harbor. Then the ML 349 immediately reversed its course to return to the open sea, framed by the bullets of that ship and the shooting of the land battery guns, It must be said that the German artillerymen of battery 1./43, the only ones who with their 88s could fire from Tobruk Point towards the inside of the harbour (see map), were credited with the sinking of that raft, while in reality, as Wegener's lieutenant Wegener expressed it, their inaccurate shot was so *"horrible that he could avoid being hit by turning after every bullet fall from the bow to his raft"*. However, his luck was short-lived. The Mc200 fighters of Major Avenue headed for his small hull and immobilized him in flames and explosions. Then Worledge ordered the ML 352e abandoned. Two hours later, an Italian torpedo boat, the Castore, left Tobruk and collected the survivors, and Worledge captured was transferred to the prison camp of Bari and then Sulmona. After the war he returned to Australia where he married Miss Margot.

▲ A complex of Vickers twin machine guns of the MTB 314 torpedo.

▼ Another twin machine gun complex of the MTB 314 torpedo.

▲ Two Italian Mc 200 aircraft of the 366th Caccia Terrestre Squadron. Aircraft of this type from the 13th Fighter Group, armed with bombs, participated in the attack on the British Sikh destroyer and the British light ship engaged in landing in Tobruk. The same aircraft in the page at right.

▼ "Faimiles" type motor launch. Two units of this type, the ML 352 and ML 353, used in the Tobruk landing, were sunk by the Italian Mc 200 aircraft of the 13th Caccia Group.

Even the ML 349, after collecting the crew of the MTB 353, was hit and damaged by the planes but was able to continue sailing and reach Alessandria. At the end of the war, on January 7th, 1946, it was sold to the Italian Navy. At 07:30 a 12.7 mm bullet from the Mc 200s was also hit by the torpedo torpedo MTB 308 (ship's lieutenant: Roy Yates), which had to stop with the damaged engine. When the navigation resumed, however, his fate was already marked, as we shall see. At the same time, 07:30, as mentioned, the Sikh destroyer, which had not yet sunk, was hit on the bridge by a 50 kg bomb. According to the assessments sent by the main Viale to the Command of the 5th Air Squad (general Vittorio Marchesi), and from this Superior Command brought to the knowledge of Superaereo on the morning of September 15th, its Mc 200 was believed to have obtained the following results[60]: *1 C.T. fully hitted by 4 bombs and 3 bombs near waterline sank; 4 torpedoes burned and sunk; 2 torpedo-torpedoes probably sunk in collaboration with German bombers at altitude later intervened. 3 effectively torpedoed torpedoes.*
Only one Mc 200 returned to the base hit by a strong anti-aircraft reaction. Altogether the twenty-one fighters dropped 27 50-pound bombs and fired 4,165 12.7mm caliber projectiles.
In the "Considerations" of his report, in which he claimed that the antiaircraft of enemy ships had been *"extremely violent but disordered and inaccurate"*, Viale highlighted the good results achieved by his pilots, writing[61]: *The shooting with bombs against ships in general was sufficiently precise, despite being the pilots at the first test. The accuracy of the shot was essentially due to the courage of the pilots who carried out the shot in the maximum totality at very low altitude (minimum allowed for unscrewing the safety device). Shooting with a machine gun against torpedo boats very precise despite sudden juxtapositions, significant speed and first use on the sea ... It was also found that "the torpedo boats and corvettes had on board petrol in milk arranged above deck. This explains how the enemy units were so vulnerable to our bursts and the immediate and brilliant effects obtained.*

---
60 *Ibidem.*
61 *Ibidem*

At 07:30 five Italian Mc 200 fighter-bombers of the 92nd Squadron of the 8th Assault Group, took off under the command of the pilot captain Vincenzo Sansone from Abu Aggag to carry out an armed reconnaissance north of Ras Kenays, sighted and attacked three motor torpedoes, in lat. 32 ° 30 'N, long. 27 ° 55 'N. The pilots plunged ten 50-pound wing bombs into a dive and fired 3,730 12.7-caliber machine gun projectiles, and upon retiring they found that the three ships had been hit, and one of them was on fire. It was the MTB 310, commanded by the ship's lieutenant. Stewart Lane, who remained at first immobilized, to then receive, as we will see, the coup de grace from the German planes.

Also on the Italian side, an attempt was also made to intervene with twelve S 79 torpedo bombers of the 131st Group of the 5th Air Team (major pilot Giovanni Villa), but the mission did not have the desired result. The S 79 of squadrons 279th and 284th, departed in two formations of seven and five aircraft, starting at 08:50 respectively from the airports of El Fateiah and Marsa Matruch.

Heading according to the order received for the Tobruk harbor, where an enemy cruiser was reported moving slowly towards the east, the torpedo bombers were unable to find the naval target to be hit, despite having been researched in both directions along the stretch of Cyrenaean coast between Ras Azzaz and Ras el Tin for a depth of about 100 km. After that, the S 79s landed on Derna airport[62].

Finally, a reconnaissance was carried out by two modern Mc fighters. 202, which during the flight east of Tobruk sighted some torpedo boats. Overall, on the Italian side, forty attack aircraft were used in the attack and search missions of the enemy ships of September 14th: twenty-six Mc 200 fighter-bombs (twenty-one from the 13th Group and five from the 8th), twelve S 79 torpedo bombers from the 131st Group , and two Mc fighters. 202 for an offshore reconnaissance flight.

On the German side, the first communication of the landing reached the OBB. at 00:45 on September 14th, and later Tobruk followed initially alarming information, then progressively better and reassuring until the day when Major General Otto Deindl, commander of the Germanic departments of the stronghold, reported: *"Disembarkation failed. Enemy formation from 06:00 east route. Two enemy ships are on fire"*.

In the meantime, with the secret message O.B.S. IA Nr. 9326/42 Gkdos, the German air commands of the 2nd Air Fleet (2nd Luftflotte), commanded directly by Field Marshal Kesselring, had been ordered to carry out extensive reconnaissance over the entire sea area east of Tobruk since dawn and *"to keep the air forces ready to use them, according to the results of the reconnaissance, against landed soldiers, or against units found in Umn Is Sziausc or against units returning"*.

The intervention of the Germanic planes of the 10th Air Corps (X Fliegerkorps) and of the Air Command Africa (Fliegerführer Afrika), respectively located in Greece and North Africa under the command of generals Otto Hoffmann von Waldau, with headquarters of command to Athene, and Hans Seidemann, who instead was in Fuka.

The following departments were available to the X Fliegerkorps:

- 2nd Squadron of the 123rd Strategic Reconnaissance Group (2. (F) / 123), with Ju 88 D aircraft, in Skaramanga;
- Command Squadron of the 1st Experimental Squadron from bombing, with the 2nd and 3rd Group (Stab., I. and II./LG.1), with Ju 88 A aircraft, in Iraklion;
- 2nd Group of the 100th Bombing Squadron (II./KG.100), with He 111 aircraft, in Kalamaki;
- Command of the 27th Hunting Group (Jagd. Kdo JG.27), with Bf 109 aircraft, in Kastelli;
- 3rd Group of the 26th Heavy Hunting Destroy Squadron (III./ZG.26), with Bf 110 aircraft in Kastelli.

---

62 ASMAUS, "Comando 131° Gruppo Autonomo Aerosiluranti, Relazione sull'attività svolta dal 131° Gruppo Autonomo Aerosiluranti nel mese di settembre 1942-XX".

▲ From the left, General Curio Barbasetti of Prun, Chief of Staff of the Superior Command in North Africa (Delease), and General Vittorio Marchesi, Commander of the Libyan Air Force - 5th Air Team. At an airport in Cyrenaica they await the arrival from Rome of the plane of Marshal Ugo Cavallero, Chief of General Staff of the FF.AA. Italian.

▼ The MTB 313 torpedo torch, one of the nine units of the 15th Flotilla.

The following were available to the Afrika Fliegerführer:
- 121st Squadron of the 121st Strategic Reconnaissance Group (1. (F) / 121), with Ju 88 D aircraft;
- 4th Squadron of the 12th Tactical Reconnaissance Group (4. (H) 12), with Bf 110 aircraft;
- 12th Bombing Squadron of the 4th Group of the 1st Experimental Squadron (12./LG.1) with Ju 88 A aircraft;
- Command Squadron of the 3rd Stuka Wing with the 1st, 2nd and 3rd groups (Stab., I. II. And III./St.G.3), with Ju 87 D aircraft;
- 1st, 2nd and 3rd groups of the 27th Fighter Wing (I., II., And III./JG.27), with Bf 109 aircraft;
- 3rd Group of the 53rd Fighter Wing (III./JG.53), with Bf 109 aircraft;
- Bomb Fighter Squadron (Jabo. St. Afrika), with aircraft Bf 109.

Overall, on the day of September 14th, the two German commands sent three hundred and eighteen planes in flight, of which, excluding the reconnaissance and escort fighters, they employed a total of as many as one hundred and sixty-seven offensive type aircraft on the enemy ships throughout the day: eighty-one were Ju 88 bombers of the X Fliegerkorps, seventy-three Ju 87 dive bombers and thirteen Bf 109 fighter-bombers of the Fliegerführer Afrika. They were also joined by eleven Fliegerkorps Ju 88 bomber took off from Sicily and landed at Haggard el Quesada, from where they operated against enemy ships.

Fourteen other Bf 109 fighter-fighters of the Fliegerführer Afrika were employed in attacking terrestrial targets on the front line of El Alamein, making use of a strong spare fighter cover of the same type, classified in the three groups of the JG. 27, twenty-nine aircraft which they fought a fight with about eighty enemy fighters without achieving any result[63].

On the British side we know that the combat was modest, and it took place in the morning, beginning at 10:50 am, west of El Qattara between eight Kittwhawks of the 3rd Australian Squadron, which took off on alarm, and sixteen Bf 109 of II./JG.27 , one of whom was considered probably shot down in collaboration by the second lieutenant GC Coward and Sergeant G.R. Jones. Part of the German planes, as we shall see, were unable to trace the naval targets and the others, who instead attacked them, were unable to achieve any success against naval units with a slim shape and highly maneuvering. However, tangible results were not lacking, showing the enemy how dangerous it was to push his ships into the waters under strong control by the Axis air force, in the so-called "Bomb Alley", the Viale delle Bombe, the sadly famous stretch of sea between the coast Egyptian and the Isle of Crete, British ship cemetery. But let's go in order. Starting from 06:25 and until 18:26, fourteen Ju 88 reconnaissance aircraft took off, partly destined for armed explorations. One of them attacked the destroyer Zulu in lat at 07:45 without success. 32 ° 18'N, long. 24 ° 25 'E, and two other Ju 88 of I./LG.1 (Lieutenants Wolfgang von Bergh and Ernst Leopold Wannenmacher) bombed as many torpedo boats, respectively at 09:15 and 11:32, north-east of Tobruk, to then go to land in Cyrenaica, in Haggard el Quesada. Subsequently, following a sighting of Force D that occurred at 06:37 in lat. 31 ° 55'N, long. 31 ° 55'E, 50 miles north-east of Marsa Matruh, at 09:05 fifteen bombers Ju 87 of the 3rd Stormo Stuka (St.G.3) took off from African airports, which did not sight the British ships. Then, with departure from Heraklion (Crete), it was the turn of twenty Ju 88s, of which thirteen from the 1st Group and seven from the 2nd Group of the 1st Experimental Squadron (I. and II./LG.1), which took off at 10:11 from Heraklion.

---

[63] In a fight the next day, September 15th, a particularly exciting day for the Luftwaffe fighters, Lieutenant Hans Joachim Marseille, the "Star of Africa", of I./JG.27, credited himself with the shooting down of seven enemy fighter planes, achieving 150 successes. He was at that time the most victorious pilot of the Luftwaffe, and he was decorated with the iron cross with swords and diamonds oak fronds, and with the Italian Military Gold Medal of Valour. In the following days he achieved 158 victories, but on September 20th his Bf 109 crashed into an accident and crashed to the ground causing the death of Marseille at only 22 years old. He was buried in Derna, and then moved after the war to the Tobruk cemetery.

Commander of I./LG.1 was Captain Joachim Helbig, commander of II./LG.1 Major Gerhard Kollewe, both awarded the Knight's Cross with Oak Fronds[64].

The aircraft of the two formations reached their targets in the Tobruk area, and then attacked naval units individually, including a destroyer who was deemed hit by the crews of I./LG.1. One of the Ju 88 of II./LG.1, hit during the dive by the machine gun of MTB 308 (ship's lieutenant. Roy Yates), crashed on the same torpedo torch, which was initially immobilized for damage to the machines caused by the attack degli Mc 200 of the 13th Caccia Group of the main Viale, to then resume navigation. The small unit was lost, disintegrating, with the entire crew. The four men of the German aircraft, which belonged to the 4th Squadron (4./LG.1), also had the chief of crew, the non-commissioned officer Karl-Heinz Bruns.

After at 07:30 on September 14th the team destroyers Aldenham and Belvoir left Force D to go to Alexandria at 10:45 am (11:40 am according to British reports), being north of Marsa Matruh, the Coventry anti-cruiser, the most representative ship of Force D, was the main target of a formation of sixteen Ju 88 of I./LG1, which took off from Quesada (where they had landed after the first attack coming from Iraklion) were armed, each aircraft, with a 500 kg bomb and three 250 kg bombs.

▲ Pilot Captain Joachim Helbig, commander of I./LG.1. at Eleusis in Greece. Behind him is a Ju 88 bomber being refueled.

---

64 Helbig, who reached the rank of general after commanding the 1st Experimental Wing (LG.1), was one of the most extraordinary aces of the Luftwaffe's bombing specialty. At the end of the war he was credited with the destruction of 182,000 tons of enemy ships, carried out in 480 missions, deserving the oak tree branches swords and brilliants on the honor of the Knight's Cross (Ritterkreuz), deserved on November 9, 1940, when during the operations against England he commanded the 4th Squadron of the II./LG.1.

▲ Junker 88 in version A 10 of I./LG.1 of the X Fliegerkorps operating in the Mediterranean starting from the bases of Greece, Crete, Libya and Sicily. For its operational versatility, in being used as a horizontal bomber and swoop bomber, as a torpedo bomber, and in the C and D versions as a night fighter and strategic reconnaissance aircraft, it was called "the Luftwaffe's miracle plane", as well as the Super "Stuka" for its 60° swoop.

▼ The anti-aircraft cruiser Coventry.

▲ The Coventry before he was attacked by Ju 88 of I./LG.1.

On that day on September 14th only twenty long-range twin-engine fighters Beaufighter of the 252nd and 272nd Squadropn of the RAF 201st group (deputy air marshal Leonard Slater) were available for the escort to the ships, of which only thirteen were employed. which remained in flight from dawn to after sunset on September 14th, using their IFF apparatus as a signal of recognition.

At 11:10 am unidentified planes were reported by the Coventry cruiser radar from the south at a distance of 32 miles, and at 11.15 am it was calculated that they were flying at an altitude of 4,000 feet. At that time seven Beaufighters were on ships, two at 11,000 feet, three at 8,000 feet and two at 1,500 feet, but only the three that were at 8,000 feet were able to intervene, but with the only modest result of disturb German planes.

When the dive attack began in lat. 32 ° 23 'N, long. 28 ° 27 'E. the sixteen Ju 88 of the I./LG.1 were mistakenly exchanged on Coventry for fifteen dive bombers Ju. 87 that flying in three formations directed two against the anti-aircraft cruiser and one against the escort destroyer Croome.

Coventry was hit in full by four bombs. The first hit forward, in front of the cannon station, opened a large gash on the side of the hull up to the end of the waterline and serious fires began, which forced the ammunition deposits to be flooded as a precautionary measure, except that of the complex 40mm pom-pom quadruple anti-aircraft, which was not made possible due to scraps and fires.

The second bomb, and probably also the third bomb, hit the bridge in the bow and exploded inside the cruiser's hull, demolishing the structure of the upper deck, the command bridge and the radar station room. The fires resulted in the interruption of all ship communications. The fourth bomb exploded in the boiler room destroying it, while the radar transmission room was knocked out.

Also targeted by the fire of the 20 mm cannons and the Ju 88 machine guns, with incendiary bullets, which increased the damage, the Coventry remained immobilized, and in that position, in flames, was photographed by the aircraft of the lieutenant pilot Horst Berger.

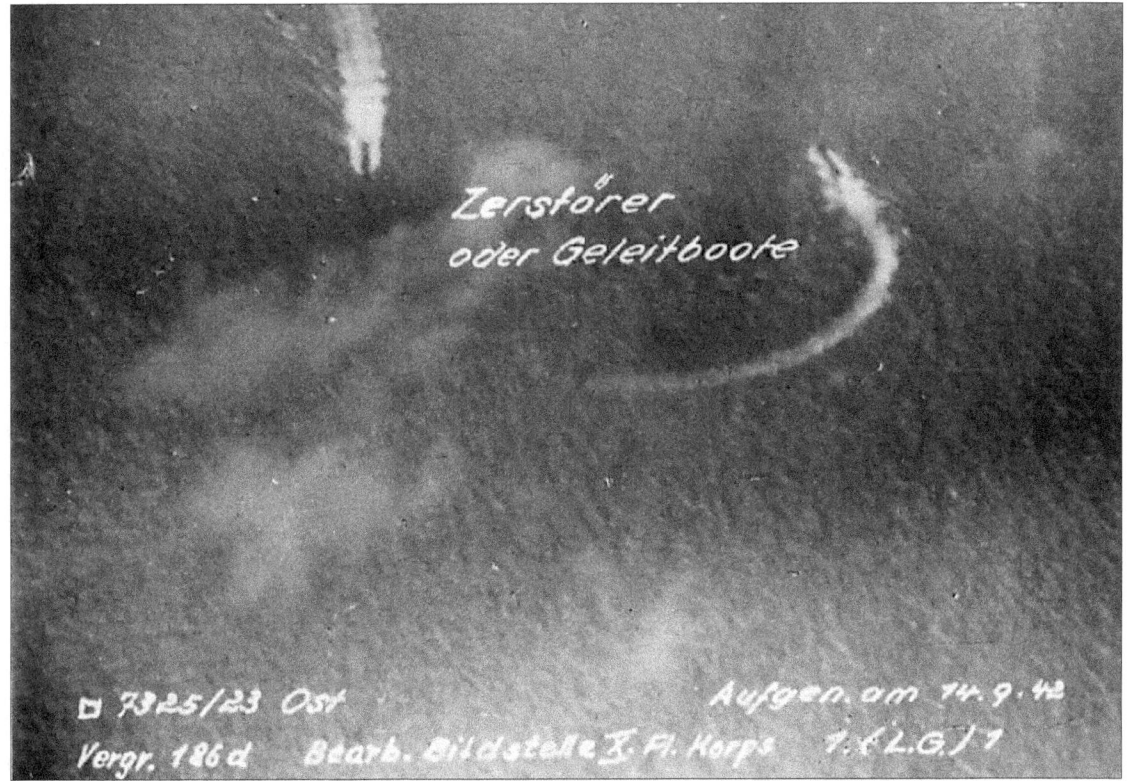

▲ 10:45 a.m. on September 14th. Two British units manoeuvred under attack from the Ju 88 bombers of I./LG.1. Some of the other photos that follow, which the author had not yet published, are absolutely unreleased.

▲ The anti-aircraft cruiser Coventry, hit by four bombs, arrested and in flames taken by one of the Ju 88 of I./LG.1 who had attacked him.

One of the Beaufighter fighters that chased German aircraft for 40 miles after the attack was damaged by the bombers' machine guns, but the pilot returned to the base optimistically claimed that he had probably destroyed a Ju 87, possibly another Ju 87 and a Ju 88, and to have attacked and damaged four more. During the attack, the destroyer Croome was not hit but had his 285 and 286 radars taken out of use for a bomb that fell near the hull, while the Coventry, after being hit by the four bombs, for the efforts of the crew was able to proceed slowly by restarting an engine. But being on fire at the bow and stern he was abandoned to avoid human losses and damage to the ships that were close to him for any other airstrikes. The escort destroyers Beaufort and Dulverton approached Coventry and recovered the crew, apart from the men who could still serve for a possible tow attempt Once the Ju 88s landed at 11.27, returning to Haggard el Quesada to refuel before returning to Iraklion, their I./LG.1 crews who had led the action reported, with considerable optimism, that they had hit the cruiser with nine bombs. They also claimed that a destroyer of the escort had been hit in full by a bomb, while two other bombs fell on the side of that ship and many others in its vicinity, noting the development of smoke in the bow. It was the Croome which, as mentioned, during the actions brought some damage to the radar for a close hit.

▲ Another image of the arrested and burning Coventry taken from another angle.

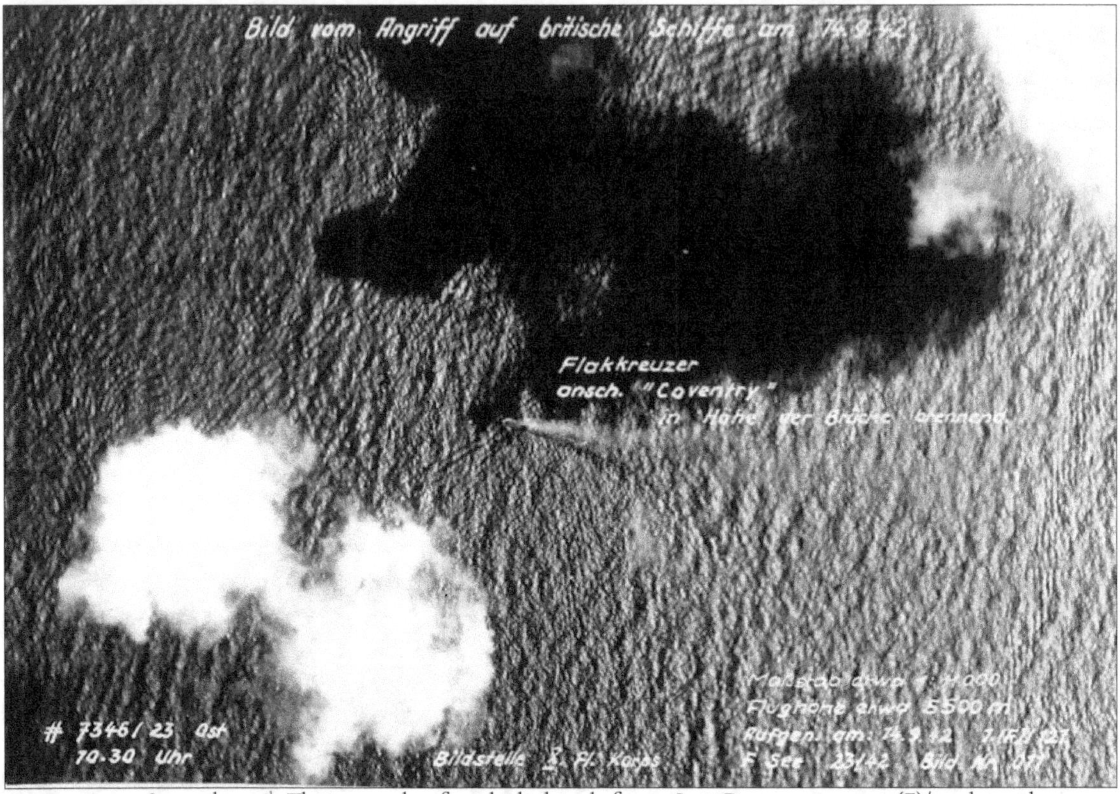

▲ 10:30 a.m. on September 14th. The image taken from high altitude from a Ju 88D reconnaissance 1.(F)/121 shows the Coventry anti-aircraft cruiser on fire.

▼ 11:52 a.m. on September 14th. A Ju 88D scout from 1.(F)/121 filmed a motor torpedo boat that was hit by a bomb. Actually, for the time of the attack, it must have been the MTB 308 that exploded after being hit by a Ju 88 of the II./LG.1, hit by anti-aircraft during the dive.

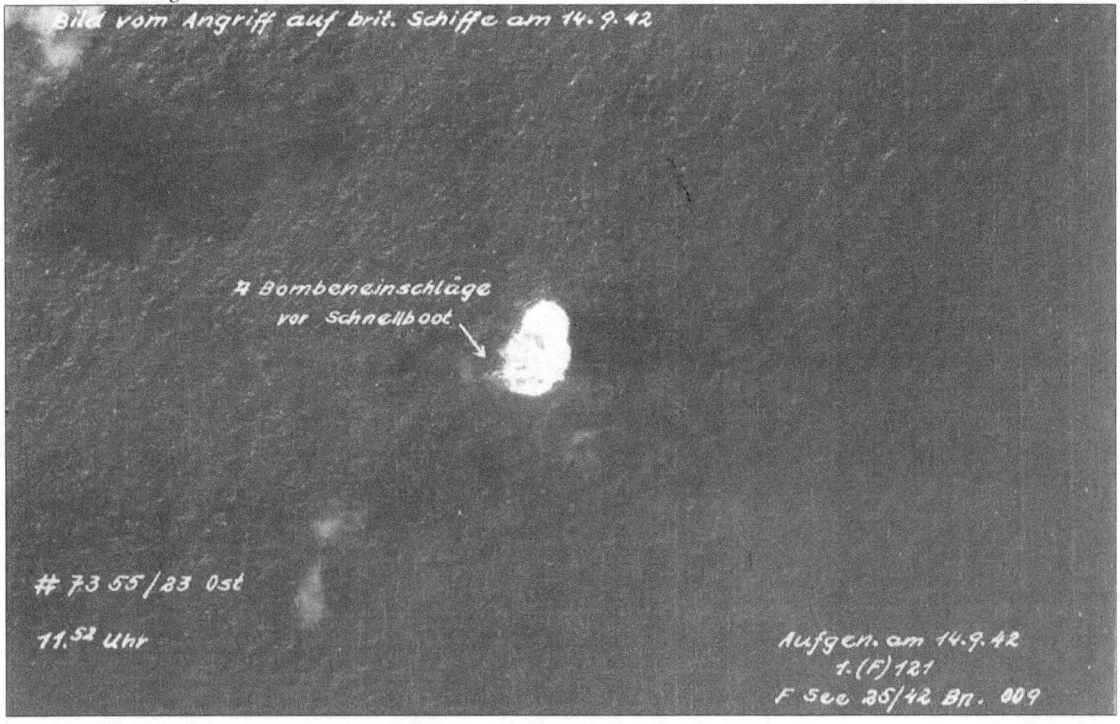

The raids against British naval units heading for Alexandria followed with increasing intensity by German planes. The destroyer Zulu, who after being missed by some bombs had received the order to reach the immobilized Coventry to give him the coup de grace with the torpedos, while sailing to the east, being in the Marsa Matruh area, was targeted from a formation of seven Ju 88 of the I./LG.1 taken off from Quesada and that between 12:06 and 12:08 he swooped from a height between 1,000 and 1,300 meters what he believed to be a small cruiser; and this because the Zulu, viewed from above, showed its six 120 mm and two 102 mm cannons arranged in four twin turrets, two at the bow and two at the stern. Ju 88 crews believed they hit that target with two 250-pound bombs and the ship's superstructures being blown up. At 12:24 the Zulu reported to Alexandria that he had been attacked by ten bombers and had not been hit.

While the Ju 88 bombers of the X Fliegerkorps were in full operation, the Ju 87 of the Fliegerführer Afrika were about to intervene, on the morning of September 14th from Sicily eleven Ju 88 bombers were sent from Quesada to Sicily, eight of the II./KG.77 (Captain Heinrich Paepcke) and three of III./KG.77 (captain Heinz Richter). The first take-off to search for British ships took place at 11:00 with the departure of four Ju 88 of II./KG.77 who returned to Quesada at 13:55 after attacking two destroyers, one of which appeared in flames, with a dive and release of the bombs from the altitude of 800 meters but without success. At 15:20 the other four Ju 88 bombers of II./KG.77 took off from Quesada. At 5:45 pm one of them attacked a cruiser and the other three two destroyers, but without success. The antiaircraft of the ships was considered strong, and there was also the attack of two Beaufighter fighters. After the bombs were released, the four Ju 88s landed in Crete.

Finally, at 15:50 the three Ju 88 of III./KG.77 took off from Quesada to attack ships marked in 6300 square, but they did not find the target and they also went to land in Crete.

▲ British destroyer Zulu.

In the meantime, at 11:40, five Ju 88Ds of the 2nd (F) / 123 had taken off from the Crete airports, leaving for sea reconnaissance south of the island, followed by six other Ju 88s for the same task, at 2:20 pm. Attacks then began from the departments of the Fliegerführer Afrika, which employed fifty-eight Ju.87 aircraft of the St.G.3 (Lieutenant Colonel Walter Sigel) throughout the afternoon of September 14th, two of which belonged to the 2nd Group (II./ St.G.3), commanded by Captain Kurt Kuhlmey, fell completely destroyed by collision on the airport of Haggag el Quesada; incident that resulted in the death of the four crewmen, pilots Lt. Jacob Konig and Petty Officer Josef Jaumann and their machine gunners.

The first two formations of the St.G.3, each consisting of fifteen Ju 87 aircraft, took off at 05:40 and 09:05 respectively; the first for an offensive reconnaissance in the sea area between Marsa Matruh and El Alamein; the second to attack a naval formation. Both did not spot the target.

The formation that followed with departure at 12:05, consisting of eight Ju 87 aircraft of the St.G.3, attacking in the early afternoon hours managed to achieve a useful result against one of the torpedo boats, sinking it north of Marsa Matruh.

It was the MTB 310 (ship's lieutenant. Stewart Lane), which at 07:30, as we said, had been seriously hit by the Mc 200s of the 8th Hunting Group. The German crews found that the small ship was loaded with soldiers, who, together with the crew members, escaped reaching the African coast.

▲ In a Libyan base a Ju 87D of the 6th Squadron of the II./St.G.3 Fliegerführer Afrika.

Also in the early afternoon, Zulu was the main target of the Luftwaffe. At first he was attacked by nine Ju 88 bombers of II./LG.1, led by captain Karl-Heinz Schomann, who, however, failed to score. According to the report of the OBB. one of the Ju 88 of the 6th Squadron (having been attacked and hit by a Beaufighter fighter of the RAF 252th Squadron with pilot Sergeant SJ Kernagham), ended up at sea, because the pilot, non-commissioned officer Karl-Heinz Mattaei, was forced to carry out a forced ditching 30 km north-northeast of Cape Kenays; and another Ju 88 of the 4th Squadron, with pilot Lieutenant Alfred-Peter Auer, was shot down for error of recognition by the German anti-aircraft while landing in Haggag el Qasaba. It was the third aircraft of the II./LG.1 to be lost that September 14th.

But it was destined that a fatal epilogue would occur for the destroyer, and it began immediately after the crew had abandoned him, and in part had been recovered by the escort destroyers Beaufort (Lieutenant of Standish O'Grady Roche vessel) and Dulverton (corvette captain William Napier Petch). To give the cruiser the coup de grace, Beaufort fired several shots at Coventry with little effect. Then the Croome intervened (corvette captain Rupert Cyril Egan) who, being in the company of Hursley (vessel lieutenant. William John Patrick Church), stormed the cruiser with one hundred and twenty-four projectiles, and then attempted to finish his task by detonating at the hull of that ship three depth bombs, but also unsuccessful. Back then, the Croome reported that the burning Coventry was still afloat although it had been fired at artillery and depth charges. The Zulu was then warned to go and give the cruiser the coup de grace and therefore the destroyer headed for Coventry, to complete the thankless task entrusted to him.

▲ A burning torpedo boat photographed at 12:36 p.m. on September 14th by a Ju 88 scout from 1.(F)/121. It was probably the MTB 310, which after being severely hit by the Mc 200 fighters of the 8th Group had been hit and sunk in the early hours of the afternoon by the Ju 87 of St.G.3 north of Marsa Matruh.

▲ German Bombers JU 88 of 5ᵗʰ Squadron II./LG.1. During the operations this bombing group of the 1ˢᵗ Experimental Wing of the X Fliegerkorps lost three aircraft.

▼ British long-range hunting Beaufighter of the 252ⁿᵈ Suquadron of the RAF Middle East, with desert camouflage. It was one of the mythical aircraft of the Second World War, because it was used with extraordinary efficiency both as a day and night fighter aircraft, attack aircraft to naval units and land targets, with the use of machine guns for bombs and rockets, and also in the airborne version, obtaining sometimes resounding successes in every field.

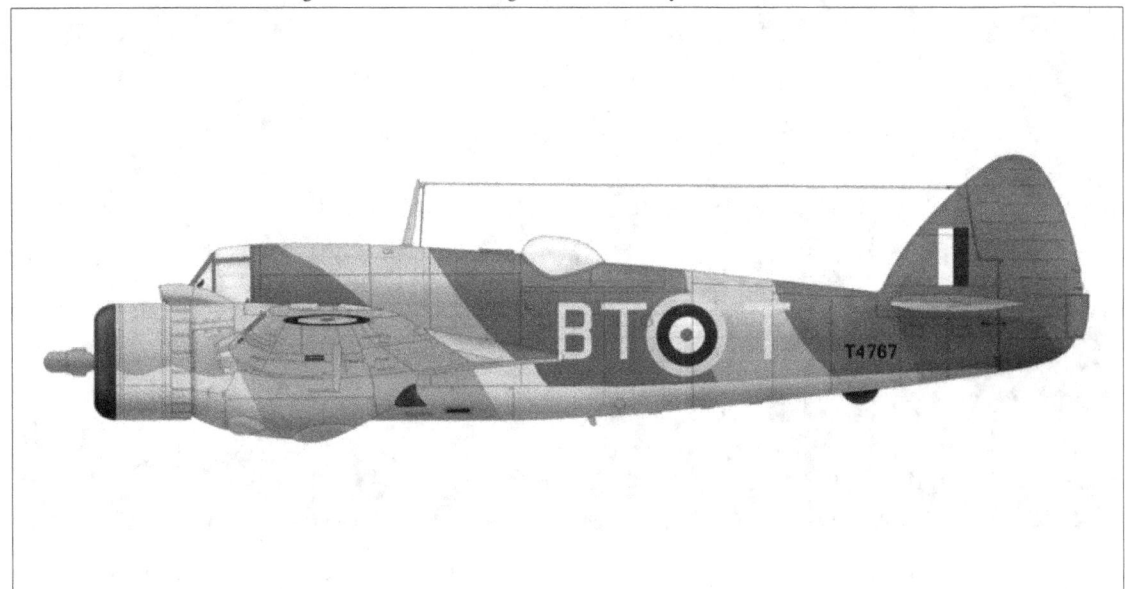

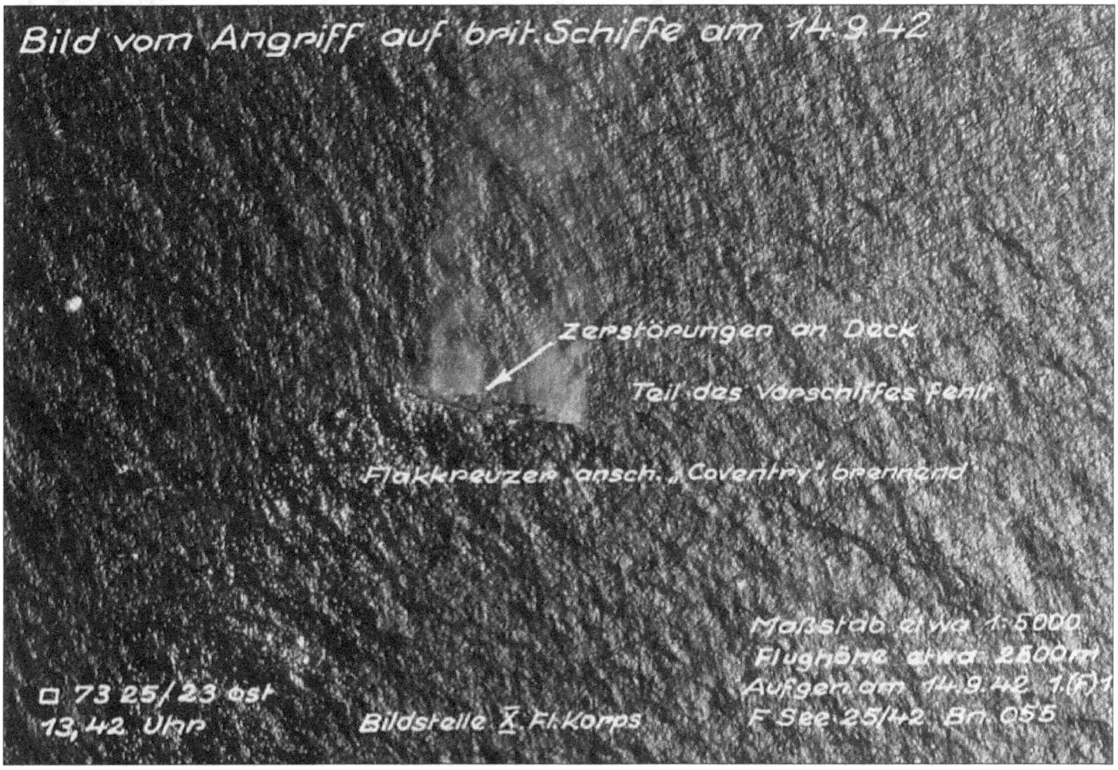

▲ The flaming Coventry cruiser photographed from high altitude, at 13:42 on September 14th, from a Ju 88D of the 1.(F)/121. The two photos are similar but different in the coloration of the print, and for the addition in the first photo of the writing below with the dates September 29th and 30th, 1942.

At 3:15 pm the Zulu reached the immobilized anti-aircraft cruiser and gave Coventry the coup de grace with the launch of two torpedoes[65].

The Coventry, with which the commander, captain of vessel Ronald John Robert Dendy, and sixty-four men were lost, sank in the evening, at 7.15 pm, in lat. 32 ° 40 'N, long. 28 ° 17 'E, in a sea area where the depth is 2,500 meters.

But starting from this moment, having remained the most representative British naval unit, the Zulu was the main target of the Ju 88 of the 1st Experimental Wing, and of the Ju 87 of the 3rd Stormo Stuka. Let's see how it unfolds.

Out of twenty LG.1 bombers that took off between 13:55 and 17:50 from Crete's airports in four formations, only the first, with seven I./LG.1 aircraft, tracked the target to attack. The bombers beat on retreating British units, which reacted to the attacks by shooting with all their weapons. Nonetheless, the Zulu suffered some damage from a bomb dropped near the hull, which caused the destroyer to slow down and put radio equipment out of use. The Zulu and also the Dulverton (corvette captain William Napier Petch) at 14:47 and 14:49 reported that they had been attacked by planes, but that they had not been hit.

Particularly exciting was the story that the crews of the seven Ju 88 of I./LG.1 made in their reports on returning to the base, as appears in the bulletin of the OBS, in which it is reported that three destroyers were hit in the attack, of which *"one on fire was seen stopping. Another destroyer hit with a 500-pound bomb and a 250-pound bomb in the mid-hull was seen stopping in flames. Another destroyer hit by two 250 kg bombs on his side and certainly damaged*[66]*"*.

▲ A Ju 88 bomber of the 1st Experimental Group Command Squadron (Stab./I./LG.1) in flight over the sea.

---

65 At 2:10 p.m. on September 14th, the destroyer Croome, who was in the company of the Hursley, transmitted that the "stubborn" Coventry in flames was still afloat although he had been shot at artillery and depth charges.
66 ASMAUS, "Bollettini operativi giornalieri della 2a Luftflotte", fondo SIOS.

▲ The immobilized Coventry that has the destroyers Zulu, Beaufort and Dulverton close by.

▼ Another shot of the Coventry, close range, before being sunk by two Zulu torpedoes.

The eastward navigation of Zulu and the two escort destroyers Hursley and Croome had a fatal end during that afternoon of September 14th. A first action assigned to three Bf 109F fighter-fighters from Stormo Africa (Jabo.St.Afrika), which took off at 13:15 to attack the naval formation, was unsuccessful due to the failure to sight the target.

Subsequently, the three British ships were attacked by a formation of eight Ju 87 of the St.G.3 took off at 13:35 from Haggag el Quesada. The Stuka pilots noticed many bombs falling near the hulls, but without hitting direct targets.

Then, at 15:30, another formation of dive bombers arrived on the same target, also taken off from Haggag el Quesada, consisting of nineteen Ju 87 of the 3rd Group of the 3rd Stormo Stuka (III./St.G.3 ex II./St.G.2), and led by the department commander, Captain Kurt Walter. The pilots, who returned to the base, declared that they had hit a destroyer with a 250 kg bomb, on which a large fire developed.

In fact, at 4:15 pm according to British time, the bomb exploded in the engine room of the Zulu, causing the flooding of the boiler rooms and machines, and stopping their speed. The destroyer, having landed the soldiers who were still on board, transferring them with almost all the crew on the Croome, which embarked nine officers, one hundred eighty sailors and sixty Royal Marines, was towed by Hursley (vessel lieutenant. William John Patrick Church). But since the Zulu's buoyancy was compromised by the strong water entering the hull, the destroyer was definitively abandoned, even by the core of the men who had remained on board for towing operations.

▲ The pom-pom squared anti-aircraft complex of the Zulu destroyer.

▲ German fighter Bf 109F in "Jabo" configuration (fighter bomber). Note the 250 kg bomb under the nacelle.

▼ Fighter-bomber ("Jabo") Bf 109F of Wing JG.27 in Libya-Egypt.

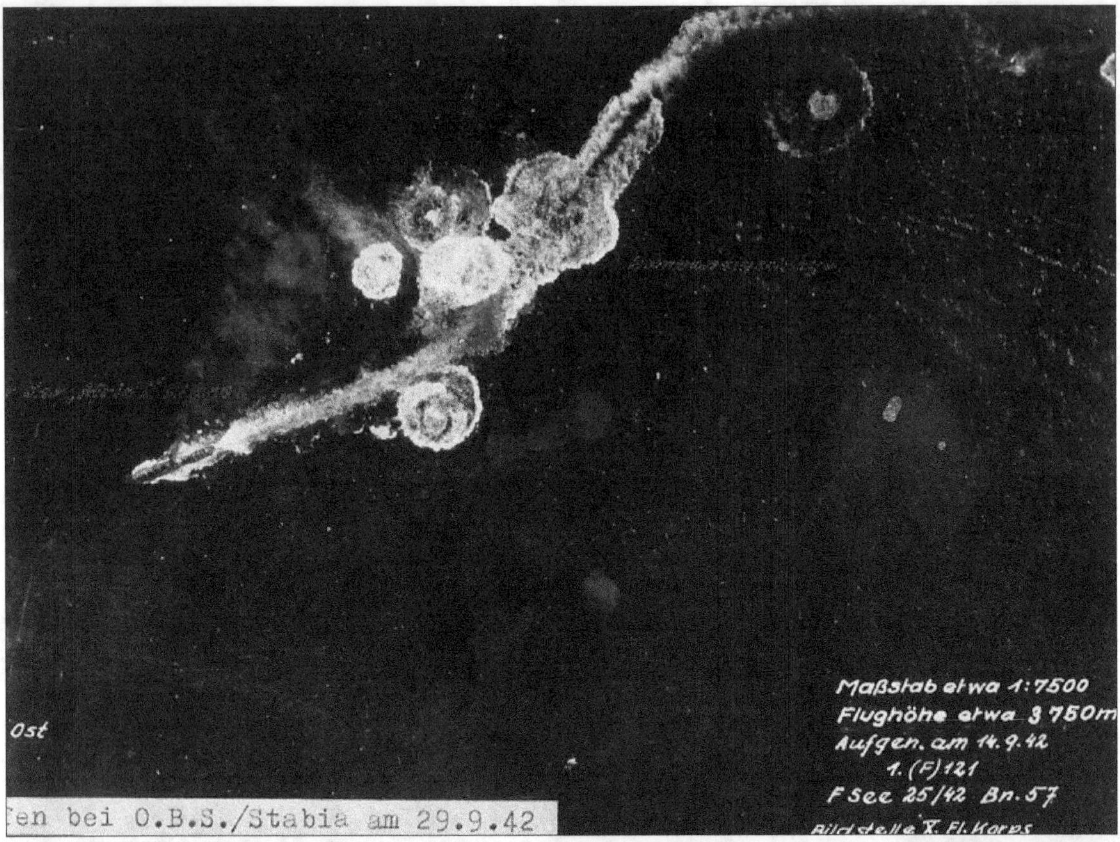

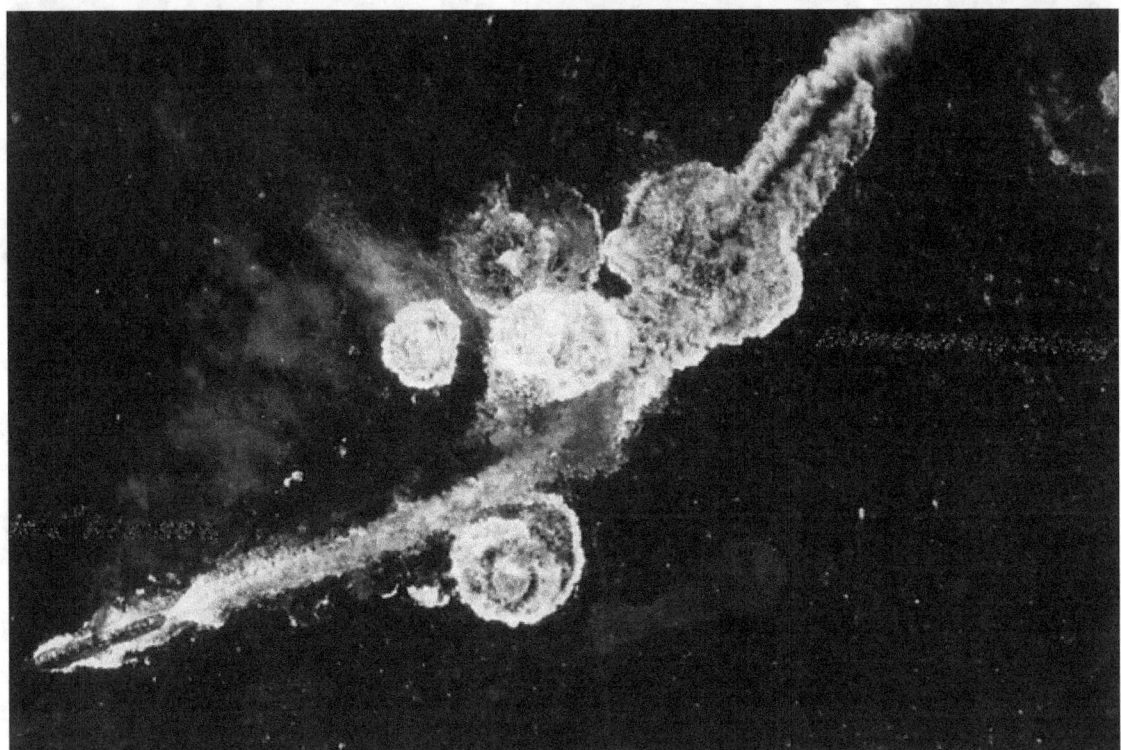

▲ The Zulu destroyer manoeuvres to dodge the bombs dropped by Ju 87 of III./St.G.3. The photo (below enlarged) was taken from a Ju 88D reconnaissance squadron 1.(F)/121.

After an attack by nine other Ju 87 of the St.G.3 arrived on the surviving ships at 16:45, whose crews believed they had seen a 250 kg bomb explode near the side of a destroyer, on the German side in the late afternoon, between the 16:00 and 17:50, thirteen Ju 88 of the LG.1 of the X Fliegerkorps were still sent in flight, took off from Crete in three small formations, fourteen Ju 87, and twelve Bf 109 fighter bombers of the Fliegerführer Afrika, also the latter took off in three small patrols.

By flying in a single formation, the fourteen Ju 87 of St.G.3 were able to carry out their mission regularly by attacking, at 17:10, four motor torpedoes, without however being able to evaluate their destructive effects. It was only damaged by the splinters of the bombs that fell near the hull the MTB 266 torpedo-torpedo boat (second lieutenant of John Norman Broad vessel).

Then followed the actions of the Jabo fighter-bombers, St. Afrika. The first patrol of three Bf 109, which left at 4 pm to attack the naval forces, did not spot the target; three other Jabo, departing at the same time, attacked a cruiser in a grazing flight surrounded by two destroyers 180 miles north of El Daba. One of the destroyers appeared hit by two 250-pound bombs. One of the two ships stopped was certainly the Zulu, with the destroyers Hursley and Croome next to it which at 17:07 reported being attacked by planes. Finally, six Jabo Bf 109 attacked the same naval formation north of El Daba, with bombs falling very close to the hulls of the targeted British units. Also in this case the Croome report, at 5:47 pm, to be attacked by bombers.

During these last actions, starting at 5:45 pm, fourteen Bf 109 fighters of the JG.27 took off with the task of being employed in the escort to the dive bombers of St.G.3.

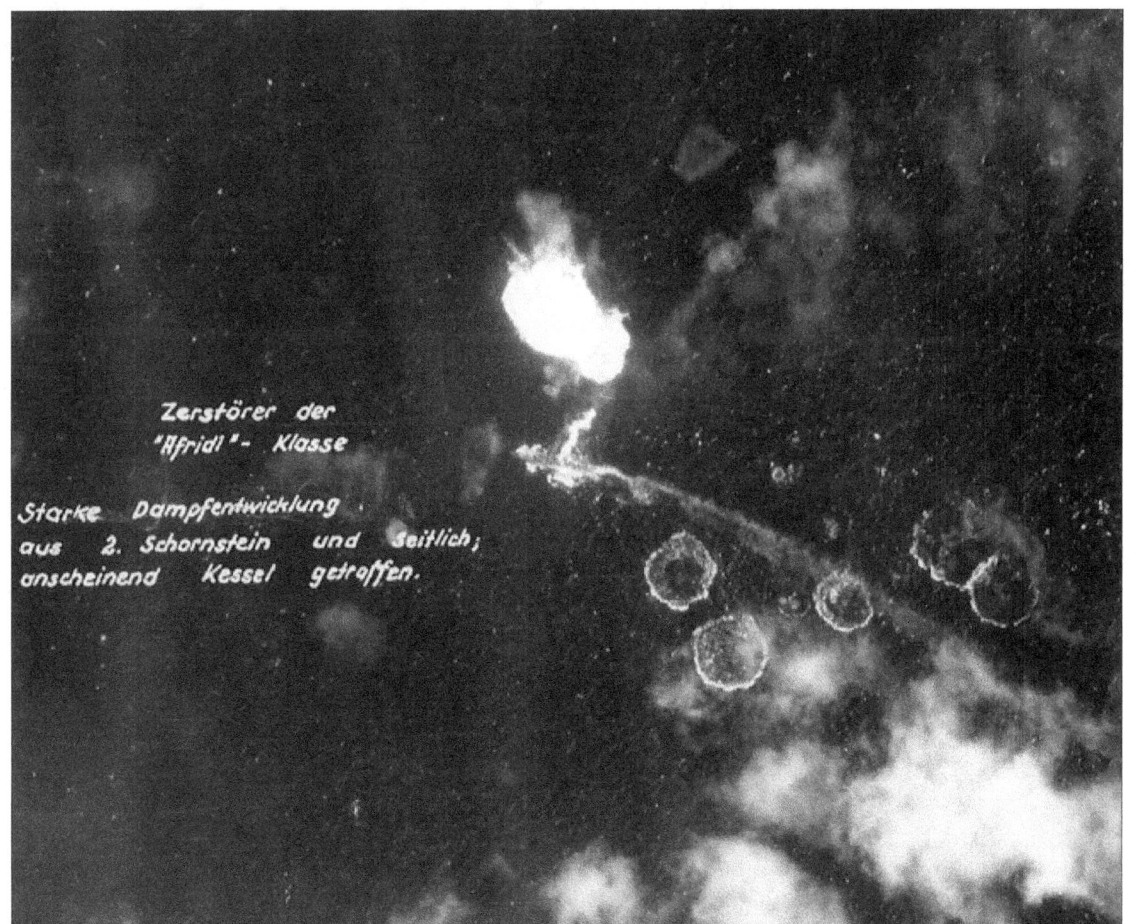

▲ Picture taken from a Ju 88D reconnaissance 1(F)/121. Time (German) 15:01, the moment when the Zulu, rightly recognized for destroyers of the "Afridi" class, is hit by Ju 87 of the III./St.G.3.

In the meantime, at 5:23pm on September 14th, the Command in Chief of the Mediterranean ordered the escort destroyers of the 5th Flotilla Dulverton, Beaufort, Hurworth, Exmoor (which already at 09:30 had signaled the cruiser Coventry to remain with an autonomy of eighteen hours to speed of 19 knots and needed oil) to return to Alexandria. Shortly thereafter, at 5:35pm, it was reported to Aldenham that the Zulu had been hit and arrested in position 032 ° 37 'North 028 ° 30' East, and that Croome and Hursley remained with the Zulu, while the other escort destroyers were returning in Alexandria. Aldenham was ordered to proceed with the rescue tug Brigant, who sailed from Alexandria, to go to assist the Zulu, and was informed that the fighters of the 252nd Wing (Flock) would ensure that ships were protected until dark.

The German air actions of the day ended with the missions of thirteen Ju 88 of the LG.1, which took off from Crete in three formations at 17:20, 17:48 and 17:50, and consisted of four, six and three aircraft respectively. But due to the onset of darkness, only the first four Ju 88s were able to track down the target. One of them, at 6:15 pm swooped into a cruiser, which was always the Zulu which proceeded with a speed of 2 knots, with the Croome and Hursley nearby. Then, at 19:30, the other three aircraft of the formation attack, always in a dive, the three destroyers, of which two appeared stationary, without obtaining results, also because the attack was disturbed by British long-range Beaufighter fighters, four of which were found in two sections at high and low altitude, respectively at 14,000 and 1,500 feet.

The Croome signaled the attack at 19:28. Two of the six Ju 88 aircraft of the second formation, having not found the ships, went to drop the bombs on enemy targets of the Egyptian coast, respectively east of El Hamman and on the airport of Burg El Arab. During the missions for the protection of ships by the RAF Beaufighters, Sergeant S.J. Kernaghan, piloting an aircraft of the 272nd Squadron, credited himself, with great optimism, the shooting down of a Ju 87 and the probable shooting down of a Ju 88. The commander of the destroyer Croome also claimed to have shot down a Ju 88, but he was a illusion. After dark, at 9:54 pm, the Zulu, skidding on the starboard and capsizing, quickly sank in lat. 32 ° 00 'N, long. 28 ° 56 'E, north of Marsa Matruh. This occurred before the rescue tug Brigant, sent from Alexandria, had been able to intervene, escorted by the escort destroyer Belvoire (to which afterwards the order would have been added to the Aldenham) and by the long-range fighter aircraft Beaufighter of the 252nd and 272th Squadron of the RAF. Thirty-eight men were lost with the Zulu, including four officers. After which the Croome signaled that he was returning to Alexandria, and that he had nine officers, one hundred and eighty sailors and sixty Royal Marines on board[67].

▲ The escort destroyer Aldenham in 1942.

67 On September 14th, the four German submarines U-371, U-375, U-559 and U-561 were located in the Eastern Mediterranean, in the stretch of sea between Alexandria and the coast of Syria-Palestine. Believing that the British ships retreating from Tobruk were headed to Alexandria and Haifa, at 17:00 the order was given to U-559 and U-375 to move to a suitable position to intercept them towards the two ports, but the two submarines did not make any sighting.

▲ From the author's article, Il falliito sbarco inglese a Tobruk of September 14th, 1942, printed by "Il Giornale d'Italia" on January 7th, 1987. E.C: The Ju 88 of the I./LG.1 that sank the Coventry left from el Quesada.

▼ On the left, Major Walter Sigel, commander of St.G.3. On the right, Majorw Gerhard Kollewe, commander of II./LG.1.

The "Daffodil" operation of the "Agreement" plan practically ended at 07:05 on September 15th, when the destroyer survivors arrived in the port of Alessandria, landing the wounded and other survivors of the ships. One of the most damaged torpedo boats, the MTB 313 (second lieutenant of the vessel. Thomas George Fuller), miraculously arrived there, although the engine room had been seriously affected by the strafing of planes. Damage of some importance had also reported the MTB 266 of the second lieutenant of vessel Richard Smith, due to the splinters for a bomb exploded near the hull, dropped by a German Stuka, who killed one of the passengers: the lieutenant R. MacDowall of the Argyll regiment.

▲ Bristol Beaufighter of the 272 Squadron of the RAF Middle East, which in Operation Agreement, starting from Egyptian bases, were intensively employed for the protection of British ships.

THE CRYPTOGRAPHIC INFORMATION OF THE ULTRA ORGANIZATION

Among the many decryptions of the ultra, in his London office in Bletchley Park, which concerned news of all kinds on what the intentions of the Italians and the Germans were, but which at the moment could not be exploited in real time, because for the decryptions they served several hours, there were two that proved important to the British. And this is both to know the fate of their captured ship, and to know that the operational order of the "Agrerment" operations had fallen into the hands of the Italians, and that the information contained therein, of great importance for knowing the movements and the targets of the British desert cores, whose operations were still in progress, and could be suspended, were passed on to the Germans.

At 10:04 on September 14th the 6th German motor torpedo flotilla informed the German Navy Command in Italy of the capture of a torpedo torch, and the Ultra, intercepting and deciphering the message, transmitted the information at 9:15 pm on 15th (ZIP / ZTPGN / 595). The second part of the message occurred with the transmission at 1:00 pm on the 14th, and the Ultra could specify that the MTB 314 had been captured by the German minesweeper R 10 of the lieutenant of vessel Merks [sic], and that it had been brought to the dock of the port of Tobruk with slight failures and with thirteen prisoner crewmen. The Ultra told the news at 13:03 on September 15th, and at the same time from the precise decryption of a series of messages broadcast by Italian and German radios, he was able to know also the losses suffered by the enemy: eight dead and nineteen wounded the Germans, fifteen dead and forty-three wounded the Italians. Losses which, however, later turned out to be much less than reality. On the same day of September 15th, the Ultra deciphered another Italian message sent by Marina Tobruk to Rome, which informed of the capture of the MTB 314 torpedo torpedo. The message reported that the Germans asked to insert that prey in their 6th Flotilla as an antisom , to replace one of their units [the R 9] in the North African operations, which had been lost (ZIP / ZTPGN / 733 and 598). In another German message of September 15th, it was specified that the capture of the torpedo torch had taken place after the resistance of the crew had been won, and that the MTB 314, slightly damaged, was under control. (CX / NSS / ZIP / ZIPGN / 594)

In another message on day 16th, Admiral Lombardi, Commander of the Navy of Libya, replied that he had no objection that the 6th minesweeper motorcycle flotilla came into possession of the British motor torpedo torch, but that the decision was to be taken by the Italian Naval Command [Supermarina] (ZIP / ZTPGM / 610). Even Delease [the North Africa delegation led by General Curio Barbasetti of Prum], while agreeing to hand over the unit to the Germans, who had captured it, replied that the decision was up to the Supreme Command instead.

On September 16th, again through Ultra, the British learned that the torpedo torch had been granted to the 6th minesweeper motorcycle flotilla, and on the 20th they knew that the name assigned was RA 10 (ZIP / ZTPI / 17385). In addition to this, the British learned, again from Ultra, that two MLC landing craft and four motorboats had been captured, and that the Navy Command in Derna asked Supermarina to send experts from Italy in order to take advantage of the opportunity who offered to study the characteristics of those vehicles (ZIP / ZTPI / 21/9/42).

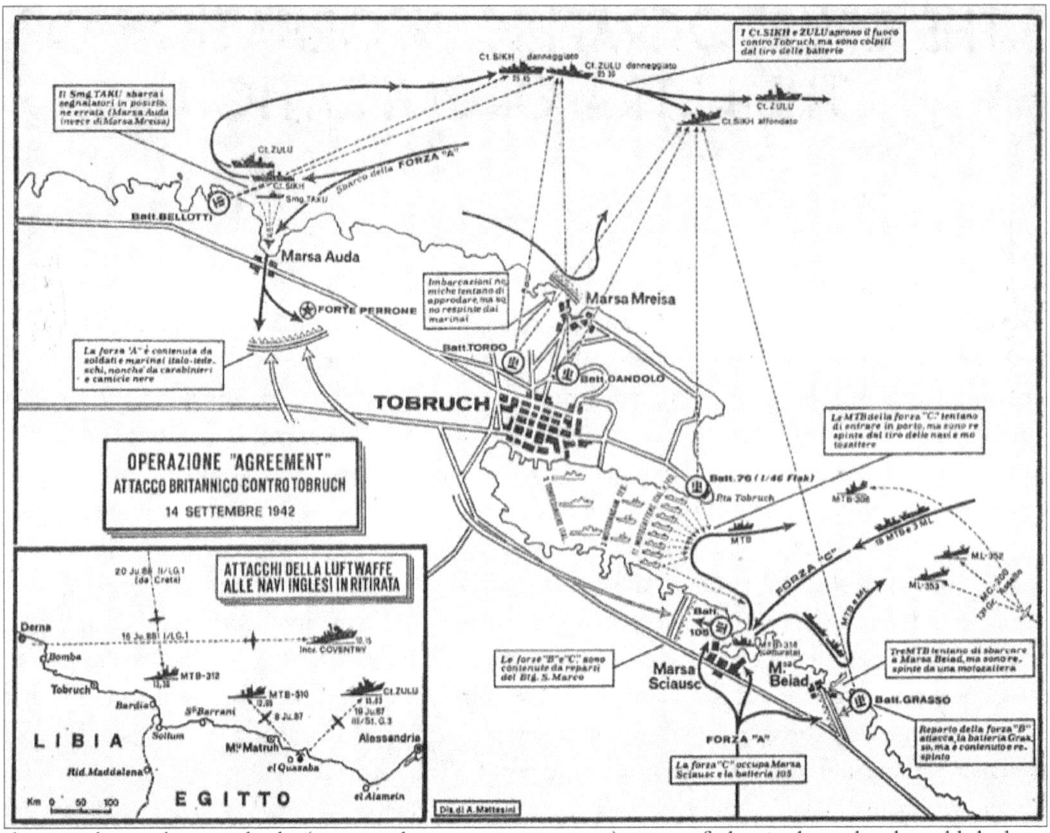

▲ The British attack on Tobruk. (Drawing by Antonio Mattesini). Map of the Author, already published in the book *La partecipazione tedesca alla guerra aeronavale nel Mediterraneo (1940-1945)* in 1980, and then printed by "Il Giornale d'Italia" on 6th and 7th January 1987 in the article Il fallito sbarco inglese a Tobruk of 14th September 1942, and finally printed by USMM, in the essay, also by the Author", L'Operazione "Daffodil" in the plan Agreement.

▼ Admiral Giuseppe Lombardi reprised in North Africa together with a group of Italian and German officers.

Let's now pass to the branching of other decryptions. On September 14th, from a German interception of 23:48 hours sent by the Transport Command North Africa to the major German commands, including the O.B.S. (TO 10510/14/9/42) it was learned that the importance of an exact enemy document was being assessed, and the following day, September 15th, the Ultra revealed that by a communication sent by Marina Tobruk to the Command Marina Tripoli, they learned that an important document captured in the port of Tobruk was sent flying to Tripoli. (ZIP / ZTPI / 17334).

Then at 19:55 the Naval Command of Tobruk informed the Marine Command Tripoli that it had the entire British order of operation which described the coordination of the naval and land forces that had invested the stronghold of Tobruk. It was pointed out how important the document was to know the actions in the desert of the various British formations with the forces employed, and it was specified in the message that the enemy had the intention of remaining in Tobruk to carry out the destruction only twenty-four hours. (ZIP / ZTPI / 17334).

Among the decryptions of the Ultra, which continuously deciphered the communications of the major Italian and German Commands, up to having knowledge of the daily reports of the various operations of the three Axis armed forces, that same day 15th was brought to know that in the port of Tobruk had been hit slightly by a 120mm bullet by the Italian steamer Sibilla, while a second shot on the ship did not explode. Furthermore, 566 British prisoners had been made, including 34 officers and an American journalist, and that 466 of them had been recovered at sea from sunken ships. (ZIP / ZPTI / 1727 and 1728).

Also on September 15th, at 06:00 a report by Supermarina on the naval situation was deciphered by the British at 14:00 on 14th, in which, among other things, he reported that against the British ships in retreat "The air attack was carried out by the Luftwaffe during the day, as a result of which the enemy was scattered and withdrawn externally in small isolated groups of varying strength".

At 7:45 pm on the same day 15th, Admiral Lombardi sent the following message, intercepted and decrypted the day after by the Ultra:

From Tobuk to Rome - From Naval Command in Libya: 28178 - Marshals Kesselring and Rommel and General Barbasetti gave a conference today on Tobruk's action last night. I made a report on the operation that I directed as Commander highlighting the role played by the air forces and naval units both at sea and on land and I warmly congratulate you on the success that has been declared of great importance. (ZIP / ZTPI / 17387 - 2009/16/9/42).

Finally, at 02:12 on September 16th, the British deciphered the message 1838/15 sent at 18:38 on 15th September by the Commander of the German Navy in Italy, in which Admiral Weichold praised the lieutenant of vessel Schmidt officer to the naval communications of Cyrenaica writing:

Immediate. Through your witness initiative and vigilance reports, which had been our only data for a while to estimate the situation, you played an important role in the swift and victorious defeat of the enemy. I hereby express my particular gratitude to you and your men. (TOI 0212/16/9/42).

▲ An important role in the deciphering of German, Italian and Japanese messages, whether compiled with an encryption machine or manually, was played by the women of Bletchley Park in the Ultra organization.

THE "HYACINTY" OPERATION: THE ATTACK BY THE LRDG ON BARCE AIRPORT

The failure of the "Agreement", which without causing appreciable damage to Tobruk, caused the British, according to their figures, to lose 746 men (about 280 of the Navy, 300 Royal Marines and 160 soldiers), including 576 prisoners. To this disaster were added only modest positive results achieved in the desert against the logistical stalking in Cyrenaica, with the exception of a particularly effective attack at Barce airport (Operation "Hyacinty"), 89 kilometers north east of Benghazi, along the way coastal Balbia. The feat was carried out by British LRDG breakers, who left El-Fayum on September 2nd, under the command of Major John Richard Easonsmith, commander of Squadron B, who had been given the task of penetrating the perimeter of the airfield, to destroy the Italian bombers Cant Z 1007 bis of the 35th Wing, commanded by Colonel Bruno Borghetti, who had two groups, the 86th (Lieutenant Colonel Goffredo Marrana) and the 95th (Major Rinaldo Tieri[68]).

The raid was assigned by Easonsmith to the two patrols G1 and T1, respectively under the command of captains J.A.L. Timpson and N.P. Wilder, with a total of forty-seven men transported by twelve Chevrolet 1533X2 vans and five off-road vehicles (Jeep), to which were added to accompany the column two 10-tonne trucks of the Heavy Section that would have supplied all the fuel needed for the first 200 miles of desert (320 km). On the return, after the first week, two other heavy trucks would have supplied petrol for the return. G1 was joined by a desert war specialist, the Russian-born Belgian major Vladimir Peniakoff (called "Poskii") with two of his Arab agents from the Senussi tribe. A third patrol, the S2 made up of Rodesians under the orders of Captain John Olivery, had received the order to head over Benghazi, beyond the moving dunes of the Great Sand Sea (between Libya and Egypt), to serve, in the operation "Bigamy", to support the raid that was to be carried out against that port by the Special Air Service (SAS) of Lieutenant Colonel Stirling. During the difficult, tiring and unnerving journey, which involved the vehicles of Squadron B to travel in the sandy desert, with a relentless temperature, a distance of 1,155 miles (1,859 Km), on September 6, 800 miles from Barce, the captain's Jeep Timpson capsized, seriously injuring the officer, who throughout the mission had to hand over command of the G1 patrol to Sergeant Jack Dennis, while he and his driver were transported to a hospital by flying in a Hudson plane.

▲ Major John Richard Easonsmith, commander of Squadron B in Operation Caravan.

---

68 AUSMM, "Comando Settore Aeronautico Centrale. Incursione nemica sull'aeroporto di Barce", *Scontrri navali e operazioni di guerra*, cartella 91.

▲ Captain J.A.L. Timpson, commander of the G1 patrol, was seriously injured in the march to Barce airport when his Jeep overturned.

▼ Major Vladimir Peniakoff en route to Barce. His Jeep is armed with twin Vickers K machine guns and is loaded with gasoline tanks, fuel necessary for the long transfer.

On September 13th, the locality of Benia, about 24 kilometers south of Barce, establishing a secret base, in a final briefing it was established that the T1 patrol was to attack the airport, while the G1 patrol would attack the barracks of the Campo Maddalena barracks, 3 kilometers south-west of Barce, and the railway station south of the village.

However, the fact that an Italian observation aircraft, Ca 311 of the 131st Squadron of the 66th Aerial Observation Group, had detected their presence shortly after their arrival in Benia. In fact, in the afternoon about twenty vans were sighted in Sidi Noies, and other vans appeared a few kilometers from Gerdes el Abid. Following this, the Cyrenaic Defense Command had placed the garrisons of the Cyrenaic Gebel in an alarmed state, which was then extended to the sectors of Derna and Agedabia-Gialo. As a result, surveillance at Barce airport was considerably increased, bringing a company from the Superga Army Battalion from Derna, and taking measures that, among other things, involved building an external and internal defense system with nine tanks type L 3/35 also arrived as reinforcement.

After the two Arab agents sent for exploration had not returned, Squadron B began to move at dusk, cutting the telephone wires along Via Balbia, and then heading to attack Barce airport; but in this approach phase two trucks collided, and one remained unused and was abandoned.

The march continued meeting an Italian motorized column in transfer; but the men of Squadron B were camouflaged with German uniforms and could continue to move forward undisturbed, to then achieve the objectives assigned in the early hours of the morning of September 14th, with Major Easonsmith who, as scheduled, developed a diversion in the city of Barce che cnino, according to his statements, with the destruction of ten trucks, a tanker and a tractor, which were in a parking area.

The T1 and G1 patrols, with New Zealanders and guards, proceeding with the lights on, to make

▲ Operation Caravan. Untira III, the Chevriolet of Captain Nick Wildere, commander of the T1 patrol in the attack on Barce airport.

the opponent believe they are half friends, left behind one of the trucks with radio equipment at a crossroads just outside Barce, after splitting they attacked the'airport. A Jeep and three trucks, with Sergeant Dennis, headed left towards the barracks, while a Jeep and four trucks, with Captain Nick Wilder, moved to the right. Then the New Zealanders started firing, hitting the planes parked in the airfield with the rapid shot of the Browning single machine guns and coupled Vicker, and targeting the barracks with a half armed with 20 mm Breda cannon, of war prey, and launch of hand grenades. The rapid action ended at 04:00.

In retreating, at full speed, chased by the fire of small arms, and in particular of two Italian L 3 armored wagons which, having blocked the way out, forced the British vehicles to turn offshore, the two patrols met with Major Easonsmith , then head to Fuka. But at an Italian checkpoint south of Sidi Selim the doctor's truck was hit, with the injury of three men who were in bodo. The vehicle taken in tow, was then abandoned together with two others who had previously been damaged during the retreat from Barce airport, of which that of Sergeant Dennis, in an attempt to leave the airport for the main road, had gone hitting an L 3 tank[69].

The subsequent attack by forces of the Italian Air Force of Libya (5th Air Team), which began at 10:30 and continued in successive waves, with a continuous strafing, for all hours of light, led to the destruction of the other vans, together with two Jeeps, and injuring several men. As a result, at the end of the day of September 14th, only three vehicles out of the initial seventeen were left available for the long retreat march, with water reserves.

▲ Chevrolet WB truck with long antenna radio system. The man in the back is manoeuvring an anti-tank rifle.

---

[69] According to the High Command Diary (p. 131), the action against Barce cost the enemy the loss of *"2 dead, 5 prisoners, 3 trucks destroyed and 2 captured"*.

with reinforcement elements requested and arrived on the evening of September 13th for the sighting of some trucks south of the town of Barce, nine L 3 tanks of the 10th Company, deployed along the north-east side at 500 meters away, and nineteen 12.7 mm machine guns, of which thirteen within the airfield and six outside the Via Balbia, with the task of anti-aircraft defense. There was also an 8 mm anti-aircraft machine gun, and thirteen positions of three riflemen each, and various patrols armed with muskets and hand grenades. Furthermore, among the security personnel, partially sent to sleep dressed to be ready to rush to the assigned defense points (Colonel Borghetti retired to his home at 11:30 pm), there were two carabinieri to protect each plane, armed with musket. Despite these concerns at 01:40 four trucks with the high beam headlights on, after traveling the Gebellina Sud road to emerge on the Balbia, appeared at the entrance to the airport.

From the first half, they fired a machine-gun fire at the sentry who had asked for the password to open the bar, without hitting it because he threw himself on the ground, and raised from the bar, by the driver's companion, and entered in the field the trucks headed at full speed towards the targets to be hit, the three-engine of the 35th Wing, which were twenty-six, and the other various types of aircraft in the parking lot. While one of the trucks [that of Sergeant Dennis] *"remained in the area of the buildings and constantly machine-gunned the doors and windows to prevent the defenders from intervening, the other trucks went to the area of the deployment of the aircraft"*, and always keeping the high beam on, they continued to shoot forward and literally as they progressed in their race with machine guns and cannons. At the same time, two other trucks traveling along Via Balbia were machine-gunned the planes that were on the northern side of the airport, maneuvering in a particularly effective way.

With their discharges of machine guns placed on their vehicles (four per truck), with the high beam headlights on to illuminate the target, firing bursts of incendiary bullets continuously on the most important targets, namely the planes, they managed to hit and destroy sixteen of them. of which seven bombers Cant. Z 1007 bis of the 35th Wing, six reconnaissance aircraft Ca 301 of the 66th Group, a German S.79, a Ghibli and a Fiesler "Storch" Cicogna. In addition, six other Italian planes were damaged, two Cant Z 1007 bis bombers of the 35th Stormo, three Ca 311 reconnaissance aircraft of the 66th Gruppo, a Ro 63. A truck with a trailer and fifty-two petrol drums were also destroyed, for having set themselves on fire, and an ambulance was seriously hit, while the Italian human casualties were represented by two soldiers killed, and six injured[70]. (Another source reports three soldiers killed, fifteen injured and one missing).

They were losses less than what the men in the command believed to have caused, that is thirty-three planes destroyed and damaged instead of the real twenty-two. The British, however, according to what was ascertained by the Italians, had two deaths, nine prisoners, as well as seven trucks destroyed or immobilized, including five in the town of Barce[71]. So "the vans" - which had acted almost undisturbed because the men on guard at the airport, who had thrown themselves to the ground or hid in improvised shelters to avoid the blows, *"went out almost undisturbed on the same road traveled at the entrance on the field[72]"*, and with all their men unharmed. Considering the number of planes destroyed and those damaged, the operation, which practically knocked out almost half of the aircraft of the 35th Wing Bombing Ground, was a complete success of the commandos.

Furthermore, on the Italian side, among the twenty-three aircraft (twenty-two Cr 42 and a Ca 311)

---

70 Giuseppe Santoro, *L'Aeronautica italiana nella seconda guerra mondiale*, Volume Secondo, Edizioni Esse, Milano-Roma, 1957, p. 327. SMEUS, Diario Storico del Comando Supremo, Volume VIII, Tomo I, Diario, Roma, 1999, p. 141.

71 ASMAUS, Comando della Piazza di Bengasi, Informazioni sulle azioni inglesi nella Cirenaica occidentale, Prot. N. 01/5494 del 20 settembre 1942. *According to British sources in the attack on Barce barracks, the LRDG department lost four men and two vehicles, and later, near Zaptié, was intercepted by an Italian motorized column and had all but two trucks damaged or destroyed. The two surviving trucks were loaded with the most seriously wounded, while the other men marched on foot for 160 miles (160 km). The Italians took ten prisoners, seven of them New Zealanders, all wounded. After a year, four of the New Zealanders managed to escape from the concentration camp.

72 ASMAUS, *Comando della Piazza di Bengasi, Informazioni sulle azioni inglesi nella Cirenaica occidentale*, Prot. N. 01/5494 del 20 settembre 1942; Comando 5ª Squadra Aerea, Relazione sull'incursione di camionette inglesi entro l'aeroporto di Barce la notte dal 13 al 14 settembre., del 23 settembre 1942, Protocollo n, 3439/OP.8.

▲ Close view of a Chevrolet truck and its three Long Range Desert Group men in the desert. One man is manoeuvring with the Italian Breda machine gun, while another is ready to shoot with a Lewis. The driver has his Enfield rifle beside him.

▼ Italian Cant Z 1007 bis aircraft of the 191st Squadron of the 86th Group of the 35th Terrestrial Bombardment Wing, which was the main target of the T1 and G1 patrols of the LRDG in Barce. Seven were destroyed and two others damaged.

that starting from the morning of September 14th got up from Barce airport to attack the vans that were moving away, a Cr 42 fighter of the 47th Group of the 50th Stormo Assalto (pilot colonel Raffaello Colacicchi), with the death of the sergeant pilot Ettore Mura. The successes of the airstrikes were good, since according to a secret ciphered British report on the results of the various operations of the "Agreerment", sent by the Commander in Chief of the Middle East, General Alexander, to the British Prime Minister on September 20th, 1942, at that date losses suffered by the commandos in the Barce operation were as follows: personnel six dead, fourteen injured, six missing; vehicles destroyed or abandoned thirty three, of which eighteen of 3 tons. The Chevrolet "Te Anau II" van of the Long Desert Desert Group T1 patrol, for the Italian airstrikes during the withdrawal from Operation Caravan, was all that remained of the vehicles used in the attack on the Barce airport[73].

According to the investigation made that same day September 14th by the Commander of the Central Sector of the 5th Air Team, Colonel Augusto Bacchiani, how British trucks entered the airport destroying the planes with the use of incendiary cartridges, the airmen on guard, armed only musket, they took refuge in the trenches located a short distance from the aircraft; and they remained almost inert until the enemy vehicles, after having run around the airfield, had moved away, almost undisturbed, retracing the same road traveled on entering, leaving behind the vivid flames of the destruction of the planes. Colonel Bacchiani argued that the enemy, taking the airport staff who were in a state of slumber while unaware, had taken action on the less defended and free of defensive obstructions side, in which the attack did not was expected; and *"against all forecasts he used the common entrance for all vehicles to enter the field[74]"*.

Bocchiani's report describes, as follows, in particular what were the main defensive shortcomings of the airport and its elements[75]: *Of course the defensive organization as a whole, even as it was built, even with tanks - could not - give the sure guarantee of success against vehicles so powerfully armed, but there could have been a better defense.*

The same tanks, although located far away, did not enter the fight - while they were the only ones who could face the trucks.

The bold and lightning-fast maneuver of the British stunned everyone.

The blame for this inaction can be attributed without making mistakes to leaders and wingmen...

The first responsible for the infiltration of the British into the airport are the defenders of Barce who allowed the trucks along the ordinary "Gebelica Sud" road to enter Via Balbia.

That everyone has lacked the daring and ardor to face enemy vehicles is true, but it is also true that none of the Air Force personnel were equipped with suitable means to face such a fierce enemy.

The Commander of the 5th Air Squad, General Vittorio Marchesi, sharing the punishment proposals put forward by Colonel Bocchiani, authorized to punish the airport commander, Captain Beccara, and the inspection captain with ten days of arrests, with the motivation for the first to have been absent from the camp during the night despite the alarm in progress, and for the second to be entrenched at the first alarm, in the Command building without having the necessary defensive barriers[76].

---

73 National Archives, ADM 223/565, cifrato 1450/19th G.M.T. September.
74 Comando 5a Squadra Aerea, *Relazione sull'incursione di camionette inglesi entro l'aeroporto di Barce la notte dal 13 al 14 settembre, del 23 settembre 1942*, Protocollo n, 3439/OP.8.
75 *Ibidem.*
76 ASMAUS, Comando della Piazza di Bengasi, *Informazioni sulle azioni inglesi nella Cirenaica occidentale*, Prot. N. 01/5494 del 20 settembre 1942.

▲ A beautiful image of a Fiat L 3 wagon captured by the British in North Africa.

▼ The Chevrolet "Te Anau II" truck of the Long Desert Desert Group's T1 Patrol during the withdrawal from Operation Caravan. It was all that remained of its vehicles used in the attack at Barce airport for the Italian air attacks. To give an idea of how effective the vehicle had been in the attack on the Italian planes, look at the weaponry comprising two 12.7mm Browning twin machine guns.

THE FAILURE OF THE "BIGAMY" AND "NICETY" OPERATIONS TO ATTACK THE PORT AND AIRPORTS OF BENGHAZI AND CONQUER THE GIALO OASIS.

After the success of the "Caravan" operation in Barce, the simultaneous Bigamy operation, the British attempt to penetrate Benghazi, failed. This operation, called "Snowdrop", coordinated with an attack by US B 24 bombers, had been entrusted to Force X, made up of about two hundred British Special Air Service (SAS) soldiers, led by an LRDG patrol (the captain's S2 John Olivery), and comprising about forty Jeeps and as many 3-ton trucks, all under the command of Lieutenant Colonel Archibald David Stirling. This column of rotated men and vehicles, whose vanguard left the Oasis of Cufra on September 6th under the command of Major Paddy Mayne, was supposed to have caused the destruction of the port facilities and logistics depots of Benghazi, and to free the British prisoners who were in a concentration camp[77].

But during the approach towards the outskirts of the city, the British, before they could pass and cause damage, were discovered in the darkness at a roadblock near the crossroads of Soluch, and contained by the Italians, with immediate reaction from machine guns, of 20mm weapons and mortars that destroyed the first two head Jeeps.

▲ Two Long Range Desert Group patrols meet in the desert. Note the amount of equipment carried on the trucks. The picture is from the summer of 1942.

---

[77] Mario Montanari, *Le operazioni in Africa Settentrionale*, Volume II, El Alamein, Stato Maggiore dell'Esercito Ufficio Stoprico, Roma, 1989, p. 643.

The surprise having failed, and having learned from an Arab explorer that Benghazi was alarmed and reinforcements had been sent and the efficiency of the minefields increased, Lieutenant Colonel Stirling made the decision to withdraw, leaving two dead and five vehicles on the ground destroyed.

In the painful retreat of Force X, men and vehicles remained hidden during the day 14th in the shelter of the rocks and so as not to be discovered. However, the expedient was not successful, since on the days of 14th, 15th and 16th September, in the folding march towards the south, the column was attacked in successive waves by the Italian planes, and in the bombing and machine-gun work ten other vehicles were immobilized, and a good amount of food and ammunition were lost, and finally also the last radio[78].

133 aircraft participated in the aerial actions against the trucks in the Benghazi and Barce areas (31 Mc 200 fighters, 81 Cr. 42 fighters, 7 S 79 bombers, and 14 Ca 311 fighters), with results considered excellent especially in the area of wad Belgarden, where the explosion of trucks loaded with explosives knocked out many vehicles and caused a great number of deaths and injuries.

Two wounded British soldiers, who showed up in Benghazi on day 15th, declared that the expedition commander, who had fallen back on Cufra (actually headed on Gialo) with the few remaining means, had sent them to the Italian Command to request a rescue column for collect the wounded. Four men, left on the scene, were picked up by an ambulance, but then died in hospital from the serious injuries sustained[79].

Pilot colonel Raffaello Colacicchi, the commander of the 50th Stormo Assalto, who in a series of airstrikes against the trucks, carried out with the 46th and 47th Groups respectively deployed with their few fighters Cr 42 on the airports of El Adem and K1, wrote in his report that it was believed that about forty trucks were destroyed in the area of Sidi Erahim - Wadi Bel GHerdam - Sidi Moies - Gerbes Ahidi area, and their personnel partly killed or injured, by the machine guns carried out by Cr.42. By repeatedly acting relentlessly, they intervened *"in a chain in patrols of four aircraft flying in the right wing"*, and attacked the vans each time with two submachine guns with the sun behind them.

In these actions, in which the anti-aircraft fire of the enemy vehicles is violent, two Cr.42 of the 47th Group, which to be closer to the Oasis of Gialo (which was to serve as a base to the enemy for the return of the nuclei of trucks who in the previous days had attacked Barce and Benghazi), with the death of a pilot, Sergeant Ettore Mura, while the other pilot, Marshal Adriano Tavernelli, who launched himself with the parachute, was taken prisoner by the commando.

Many fighters returned to the starting base with bullet holes and in one of them the sergeant pilot Emilio Cieva was wounded[80].

In the meantime, the survivors of Force X had reached Kasansho, in the area of the moving dunes of the Great Sand Sea (between Libya and Egypt), and then continued north. Joined September 19th at Gialo with the Sudan Defense Force which, as we shall see, was attacking the oasis without reason of the Italian garrison, the forces of Lieutenant Colonel Stirling received enough supplies to return, with their battered vehicles, in Cufra where the injured were transferred to Egypt with the use of RAF transport aircraft.

Eventually two men were captured by the Italians in an Arab camp, reached after walking about 150 miles without food. Altogether the Stirling forces suffered the loss of twenty-five men between dead and wounded[81].

---

78 R.P. Livingstone, "Le grandi incursioni nel deserto", *Storia della seconda guerra mondiale*, vol. 3, Cit., p. 308.
79 Giuseppe Santoro, *L'Aeronautica italiana nella seconda guerra mondiale*, Volume Secondo, Cit., p. 327.
80 ASMAUS, Relazione del Comando del 150° Stormo Assalto.
81 Giuseppe Santoro, *L'Aeronautica italiana nella seconda guerra mondiale*, Volume Secondo, Cit., pp. 308-309.

▲ Officers and soldiers of the MLA are having lunch during a stopover.

▼ Lieutenant Colonel Archibald David Stirling, commander of Force X, who failed in his attempt to enter Benghazi to sabotage its port. His Jeeps and trucks reported heavy casualties during the retreat for the attack of the Italian planes.

The subsequent attack against Gialo's oasis ("Nicety" operation), in the "Tulip" code, which began at dawn on September 16th by Force Z including a commanded motorized battalion of the Forces was also a failure. Defense of Sudan, reinforced by a battery of 94 mm howitzers and by a company of 20 mm anti-aircraft machine guns captured to the Italians, in all about two hundred men with one hundred and twenty vehicles, partly protected with armor, to which was added a patrol of the LRDG to guide the gear and explore. The purpose of the "Nicety", which began on September 11th with departure from Cufra, was to take Gialo, the last Italian outpost in southern Cyrenaica, on the edge of the desert, where there was a small fort, a barracks, some buildings and a landing strip. Gialo's occupation was to take place over a period of three weeks, using Force X as the logistics base.

The Italian garrison, consisting of about five hundred men, with machine guns and two batteries of 77/28 guns, which was isolated at 1,400 kilometers from Benghazi and 650 kilometers north-west of Cufra, validly resisted the artillery fire and the British infantry attack until day 21st, when for the approach of a column of reinforcements, which moved from Agedabia at 12:00 on September 19th, led by General Giovanni D'Antoni, commander of the Pistoia Division, Force Z received from Cairo the order to withdraw[82]. The movement, which took place under the attacks of the Italian and German aviation, increased the number of British casualties in men and vehicles[83].

▲ Average Italian gunnery station. The gun is a Breda Mod. 37 8 mm, with a three-foot barrel and a plate magazine on the left side with twenty bullets and air cooling. It was very appreciated by the Italians for its accuracy and firing distance of 5,000 meters, and it was similar in performance to the German 8x57 IS.

---

82 On September 17[th,] General Cavallero left Rome for Cyrenaica to follow the situation closely. Concerned about the situation of the garrison of Gialo, after having discussed it with Marshal Bastico and Generals Barbasetti and Marchesi, he ordered that *an action with a tactical group of self-supported infantry, with armored cars, tanks and artillery, leaving from the bases of Agedabia, be mounted immediately. I recommend to General D'Antoni to hurry up, and to General Marchesi to give the enemy no respite with the air force, even by moving units from the front area..* Cfr., ASMEUS, *Diario Cavallero*.

83 Agedabia was 220 km north of Gialo, and the column that was prepared there, quite strong and balanced, was made up of the Command of the 35th Pistoia Infantry Regiment, on three battalions, two artillery groups and a self-propelled battery; three batteries of 20 mm machine guns, a platoon of M/41 tanks, a squadron of the Monferrato Regiment on twenty-one armored cars; one hundred and thirty-eight trucks for transporting infantry troops, four ambulances and four tankers. If Force Z had not withdrawn, accepting combat, the losses it would have suffered could have led to its annihilation.

▲ The Italians on the counterattack. Infantrymen with the powerful Breda 20 mm machine gun, and with the excellent armoured car AB 41.

▼ Italian tank type M 41 taken from Tobruk. A platoon of these medium tanks was part of the column sent to the rescue of the Gialo oasis.

▲ A Cr.42 fighter. Thirty planes of this type assault version were used in the truck fighter, but due to the strong anti-aircraft reaction of enemy vehicles three Cr.42 fighters did not return from missions.

▼ Operation "Big Party" (September 13-21, 1942) (from: *Le Tre Battaglie di El Alamein* di Igino Gravina).

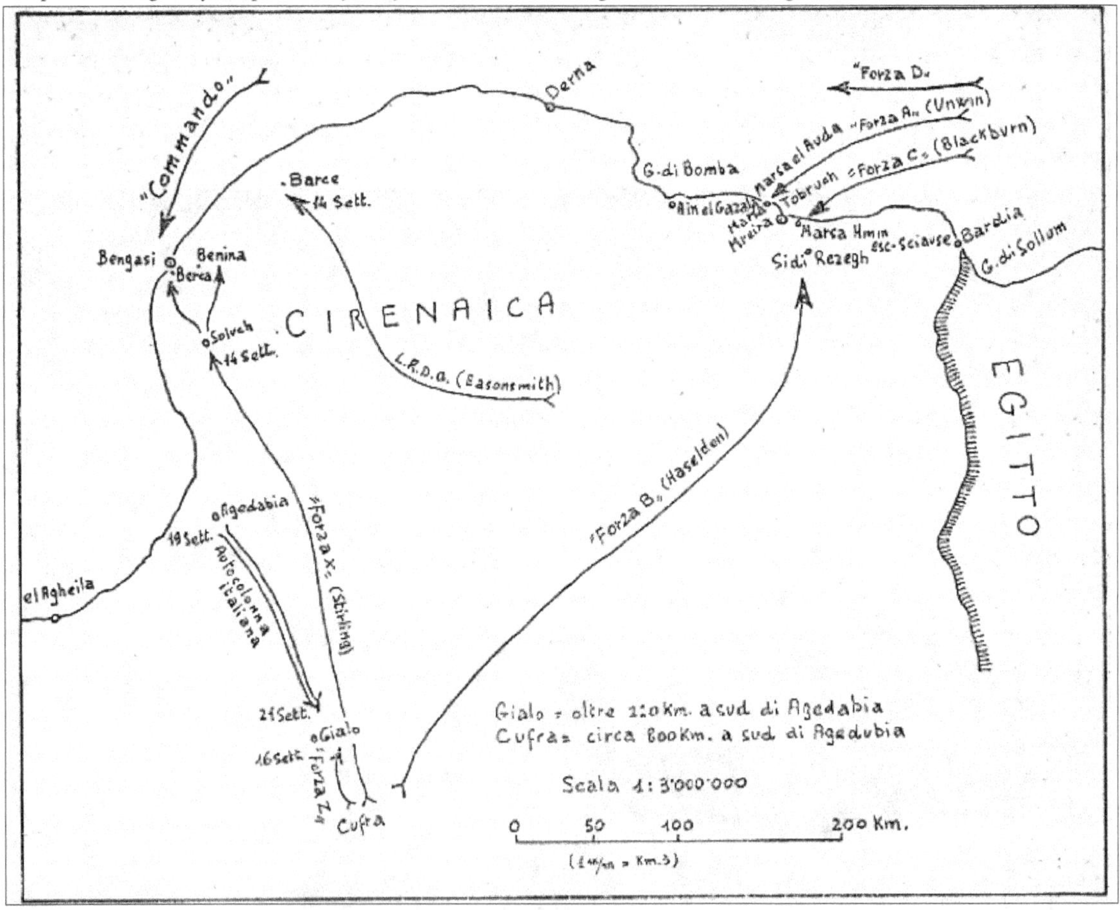

Having the Gialo radiotelegraphic station communicated immediately that the oasis was attacked and surrounded by an enemy column, the Command of the East Sector of the 5th Air Team, which had arranged for the dawn of September 16th to carry out offensive reconnaissance to continue the attacks against the British trucks that had attacked Benghazi and Barce, arranged (following a request made by Marshal Cavallero to General Marchesi) for immediate intervention in the threatened area, moving a group of twenty-five Cr 42 fighters (the 47th of the 50th Stormo Assault), armed with wing bombs, from Buerat on Agedabia airport.

During the British attack on Gialo, the air intervention took place with the use of one hundred and sixteen aircraft, of which thirty six Cant Z 1007 bis, thirty Cr 42, twenty three S 79, ten S 82, twelve Ca 311 and five "Ghibli", while the contemporary intervention of the Luftwaffe involved sixty-eight aircraft, of which, as shown in the bulletins of the OBS, several reconnaissance aircraft, five fighter bomber (Jabo) and forty-nine bombers Ju 88 of the flocks KG.54 and KG.77 of II Fliegerkorps located in Sicily and of the 12./LG.1 squadron of the Flierführer Afrika in Cyrenaica[84]. The losses of Italian aircraft were of a Cant Z 1007 bis bomber and of three Cr 42 fighter-bomber aircraft, while four S 79 returned to the base damaged and injured on board.

▲ The arrival in Cyrenaica from Rome of Marshal Ugo Cavallero with his personal plane S.79 welcomed at the airport by Marshal Ettore Bastico, on the right, and by General Curio Barbasetti di Prun, on the left.

---

84 Between September 17th and 20th, the II Fliegerkorps and the Flierführer Afrika engaged their Sicilian bombers to attack the British trucks and troops trying to conquer the oasis of Gialo. On September 17th, after a Do 217 scout ship encountered a light TRAFFIC west of Gialo in the morning, eight Ju 88s of the 12th Squadron of the 1st Experimental Wing (12./LG.1), commanded by Captain Heinrich Boecker, departed from Derna. The tactic was repeated on day 18th with two other C 217 and two Ju 88 scouts who always found a light TRAFFIC to the west and southwest of Gialo, and then intervened in the morning twenty-five Ju 88 of KG.54, whose crews reported bombing and then effectively machine-gunned some vehicles 30 km south of the Augila Oasis, observing two fires. One of the aircraft in a formation of twelve Ju 88 of the III./KG.54 (Captain Kurt Stein), belonging to the 9th Squadron with pilot Lieutenant Stadler, crashed to the ground when landing in Catania, causing 80% damage. Then in the afternoon another seven Ju 88 of the 12./LG.1 attacked vehicles in a wadi southwest of Gialo. The last action took place on September 20th and was conducted by Flierführer Afrka with a Ju 88 scout, followed in the morning by five Ju 88 bombers from 12./LG.1 who attacked vehicles, one of which was seen hit by a bomb, three others burned, and other small fires were also noted. Then followed the attack west of Gialo by four other Ju 88s, also from Squadron 12./LG.1, which, according to the crews, hit one vehicle and damaged five others.

While the Axis air force kept British forces under continuous offense, other thirty-two Italian aircraft (thirty-two S 82 and a G 12) were used, on September 18th and 19th, to transport a regiment of soldiers to Bu Amud and Derna Agedabia, where the column of troops and vehicles destined for the re-occupation of Gialo was being built. The approach of the column, as mentioned, forced the enemy to clear the oasis, retreating towards Cufra, under the attack of Italian and German planes. Even Marshal Rommel, having no news of what was happening in Gialo, and fearing that the garrison had been overwhelmed, had made rapid forces move by moving the armored cars of the 3rd reconnaissance unit of the Afrika Korps and an Italian armored personnel squadron AB 41 of the Nizza Cavalleria regiment, who had no occasion to make contact with the enemy already on the run.

▲Italian armoured car AB 41.very maneuverable in rough terrain and armed with a 20 mm cannon. From Tank Encyclopedia.

THE "ANGLO" OPERATION: THE ATTACK BY THE SABOTEURS OF THE SPECIAL BOAT SECTION ON RHODES AIRPORTS ON THE NIGHT OF SEPTEMBER 13-14TH 1942

To distract the attention of the Italians from the "Agreement" operation in the most delicate moment of its implementation, a sabotage operation was planned for the night of September 13-14th against the airports of Rhodes, Marizza and Gadurrà, called "Anglo", also intended to impair the offensive possibilities of the Aegean Air Force, in the specialties of bombing and torpedo bombers[85]. Twelve men between British and Greeks participated in the sabotage. The commando had left on August 31st aboard two submarines sailed from the Lebanese base of Beirut, the British Traveler (vessel lieutenant Michael B. St. John), of the 1st Flotilla, and the Greek Papanikolis (frigate captain Athanasios Spanidis). On the evening of September 4th, the men employed in the operation, having left the submarines, had reached the eastern coast of Rhodes, near Capo Feralco, with a foldable boat (folboat) and three boats, to then hide in some nearby caves, and rest during the first day. The saboteur team consisted of eight British elements, from the 1st Special Boat Section (SBD), commanded by Captain James Allott and Second Lieutenant David Sutherland, and by four Greeks, with Second Lieutenant Calambokidis, two of whom Pavlos Moustakellis and Antonio Moustakellis, dressed in bourgeois, served as guides and interpreters. The name of the fourth man is unknown.

After days of waiting, with the coverage and hospitality of the Greeks, spent scrutinizing the situation in the two airfields with binoculars, in order to carry out the attack with the greatest possible information, the saboteurs moved into two patrols, from a location 13 kilometers from Gadurrà and 24 kilometers from Maritza. The first patrol, directed to Gadurrà, was commanded by Captain Allott, the second, with Maritza objective, by the second lieutenant Sutherland. Not being equipped with radios to maintain contact with their Command, the patrols were instructed to return to the submarines, still taking advantage of the boats, which they had hidden, on the night of September 17-18th. Taking advantage of the dark moonless night and the cloudy sky, ideal conditions for a coup d'état, Captain Allott's patrol managed to overcome the perimeter of Gadurrà airport, without barbed wire, evading an absolutely sufficient armed surveillance and, acting for half an hour undisturbed, he managed to place the timed charges under the planes, then move away before the explosions, which began at 01:00 and ended in five minutes, giving rise to the burning of aircraft which were then completely extinguished by the tank trucks of the base at 02.30[86]. The following day, Captain Allott's saboteurs estimated that the damage that could be seen at the airport led to believe that at least twenty planes had been destroyed. Quite optimistic evaluation because there were seven sabotaged planes and of them three G 50 fighters of the 154th Group, two Cr 42 fighters of the 396th Squadron and two Cant Z 1007 bis bombers of the 194 Squadron of the 90th Group were destroyed; two other Cant Z 1007 bis, one 194th Squadron and the other of the 193rd Squadron of the 87th Group, reported damage, the first serious the second repairable in the Squadron.

---

85 About 100 aircraft were at the disposal of the Aegean Air Force at Rhodes airports (Maritza, Gadurrà and Cattavia), which included about: 30 Cant Z 1007 bis bombers of the 30th Wing (groups 87° and 90°); 15 S79 torpedo planes of the 104th Group; 50 Cr 42 and G 50 fighters of the 154th Group; and Cr 42 aircraft of the Interception Section. In addition, in Rhodes and Lero (the base of the Aegean Navy) there were about twenty seaplanes Cant Z 501 and Cant Z 506 of the Auxiliary Air Force (Marine Reconnaissance).

86 About one hundred and sixty men were present that evening in Gadurrà, including one hundred infantry soldiers and twenty Carabinieri, and more than fifty of them were on guard duty, including thirty sentries, defending the aircraft and the perimeter of the airport. At Maritza there were about seven hundred men, including one hundred and twenty-two infantry soldiers and fifteen Carabinieri, and there were at least seventy men, half sentries, on guard duty.

▲ The Greek submarine Papanikolis.

▼ The "Falboat", the folding boat used for the landing in Rhodes by the operators of the 1st Special Boat Section.

A sentry, the infantryman Camillo Falone, of the 9th Infantry Regiment of the Queen Division, armed with the 91 rifle, having heard noises at a G 50 fighter that he was watching, could have given the alarm in advance, firing a shot. But seeing in that direction a white dog attributed the engine to that presence, and did not notice the approach of two spoilers in camouflage suits who, pointing the gun, in Italian ordered him to shut up otherwise they would have killed him. He passed out of fear, and when he could recover and warn his platoon commander, second lieutenant Onofri, who sounded the alarm, it was already too late, the charges on the planes were about to start exploding[87].

The patrol of Lieutenant Sutherland, reached the Maritza airport during the night of September 11-12th, after observing during the day what the situation was and identifying the objectives, on the night of the 13th moves in two sections, the first with Sutherland and the marines John Duggan, the second led by second lieutenant Colambolidis with two other marines. The two sections moved in torrential rain, but in directing to the planes in the parking lot and a fuel depot they were discovered by a watchful sentry who started shooting, forcing the five saboteurs to flee. Their charges, exploding, destroyed a Cant Z 1007 bis bomber of the 193rd Squadron and damaged a second not seriously, repairable in the squadron, bringing the overall success of the mission to eight Italian aircraft destroyed and three damaged.

Sutherland and Duggan, although sought after by patrols of Italian soldiers, managed to reach the beach and hide. So on the night of September 17th when the submarine Traveler of the Lieutenant of St. John (who on the 5th had sunk the 1,345 tsl Italian steamer Albachiara north-west of Derna) had to collect the saboteurs, they attracted the attention with luminous signals emitted by a press, exchanging the recognition signal, and with a dinghy were brought aboard the underwater unit. The Traveler then had to dive under the attack, with the launch of depth bombs, of an Italian surveillance Mas who had sighted him. No other saboteur showed up at the appointment with the submarine, as the other ten SBD men were captured by the Italians. Those in uniform ended up in a concentration camp as prisoners of war, while the two plainclothes Greeks, having fled Rhodes in November 1941 and therefore considered traitors, were judged by a military court, which ordered the execution elder and life imprisonment for the youngest.

▲ Hunting Fiat G 50 of the 161st Group 162nd Squadron in Rhodes. Three of these aircraft were destroyed in the attack on Gadurrà Airport.

---

87 Luciano Alberghini Maltoni wrote in *Rodi Settembre 1942 sabotaggio agli aeroporti*, It. Cultura.Storia.Militare, On-Line: *The five men took between 30 and 40 minutes to sabotage 9 planes, travelled undisturbed just under 2 kilometers (round trip) in the airport area manned by 7 sentries, passed less than a hundred meters from the tents of the 1st Platoon and all this without being intercepted except by accident but without any contrast. They disappeared into thin air as they had appeared".*

The severe losses suffered by the Rhodes company, in addition to those reported by the various assault departments in the "Agreement" operation, forced the Middle East Command to dissolve the IBS, which was absorbed in the Special Air Service (SAS).

Sutherland and Duggan received the Military Cruise and the Military Medal respectively. On their venture, in 1954 a film (They Who Dare) was made with the actors Dirk Bogarde, Harold Siddons and Akim Tamiroff.

Once again, in a climate of considerable alarm for the safety of the airports and the psychological humiliation of the Italians for that attack, there was a thorough investigation opened, after an inspection of the airports, by the Governor and Commander of the Armed Forces of the Aegean, team admiral Inigo Campioni, to ascertain in Rhodes the responsibilities of those who should have ensured the safety of the airfields. Strictly interrogated officers, airmen and soldiers, having found that the responsibilities had been common, and manifested the shortcomings of the airport defense, such as that of poor surveillance, it was provided only to remove from the command of the base of Gadurrà the major Plinio Di Rollo, replaced by Colonel Achille Lorito[88].

Overall, the losses of the Royal Air Force in Barce and Rhodes by British saboteurs in the nights of 13-14th September totaled twenty-four destroyed aircraft (and of these ten were precious Cant Z 1007 bis bombers of the 30th and 35th Wing) and three damaged. If you add the five German planes lost during operations against British ships, and five Italians lost in the desert during the attack on the trucks, the number of Axis planes destroyed rose to thirty-four; that is, a quantity of aircraft that could be missing during a great air and naval battle.

▲ Rhodes 1942, during a ceremony to award medals to Air Force aviators. In the foreground the Governor and Chief of the Aegean Armed Forces (former Commander of the 1st Naval Squadron), team admiral Inigo Campioni, with on his left the division general Ulisse Longo, Commander of the Aegean Air Force, and Vice Governor Igino Faralli.

---

88 ASMAUS, Difesa Aerea, A.R.P.; Archivio Centrale dello Stato, Ministero Aeronautica, Gabinetto; Wikipedia, Operazione Anglo, Luciano Alberghini Maltoni, Rodi Settembre 1942 sabotaggio agli aeroporti, It. Cultura.Storia.Militare, On-Line.

SUPERMARINA'S CONSIDERATIONS

Thus ended the Agreement, an operation that, as General Alexander said, *"was a real failure"*. To have a successful outcome it would have had to be prepared more carefully and carried out with greater deployment of forces, as was highlighted in the aforementioned unpublished Supermarina report (see Annex 1), compiled on the basis of the British operational plan found on September 15th by the Italians on a landing craft finished on the coast.
In the "Final Comments" of this report it was, in fact, reported[89]:

1) The enemy general plan was well conceived and, if it had been fully successful, it would have effectively upset the entire logistical organization of our rear, causing a serious crisis in which the 8th Army would have benefited in its offensive.

2) The enemy plan however completely underestimated the entities and capabilities of our defense. In fact, despite having obtained the advantage of absolute surprise for all actions (what the enemy should have prudently considered as improbable), the strength capable of exploiting the initial success was lacking.

3) This underestimation is also demonstrated by the fact that the enemy had arranged the folding plan only for the success story. The lack of a fallback plan in case of failure and of provisions in the event of defense resistance have caused a serious crisis especially in the operation against Tobruk.

4) Even the use of the RAF did not foresee the case of failure of the landing, so that in the attack against Tobruk the air actions stopped entirely at 03:15, while the subsequent resumption of the actions could have contributed to breaking the resistances and to facilitate the folding.

5) Another serious element of crisis for the enemy was the error in the landing point of Force A, which made the investment in the town of Tobruk and the batteries of the peninsula miss.

6) The initial surprise was determined by the missed sighting of the Naval Forces A - C - D in the days preceding the action; as well as, as regards Force B, the insufficient supervision in the field of perimeter defense of Tobruk.

7) Finally, note the great importance that - as in Dieppe - the enemy attached to the capture of Axis landing craft.

In fact, unlike what the British thought, who in preparing their plans had underestimated the reaction capacities of the garrison of Tobruk, especially of the Italians considered "low strength fighters" and also "mediocre[90]", the Axis forces, after the initial surprise that determined a certain heeling of some defense cores, had been able to react with promptness, initiative and value . This was evidenced by the losses reported by the British marines and destroyers, who were captured almost entirely before they could have caused damage to the port works of the stronghold. The losses of the Royal Navy were also very high, since an anti-aircraft cruiser (Coventry), two large team destroyers (Sikh and Zulu), four torpedo-torpedoes (MTB 308, MTB 310, MTB 312, MTB 314) did not return to the bases and two motolances (ML 352 and ML 353).

---

89 AUSMM, "Supermarina, Operazione nemica contro Tobruk e retrovie della Cirenaica, 14 Settembre 1942-XX", *Scontri navali e operazioni di guerra*, cartella. 91.
90 Francesco Mattesini, "L'operazione "Daffodil" nel piano "Agreement". Il fallito sbarco britannico a Tobruk del 14 settembre 1942", *Bollettino d'Archivio dell'Ufficio Storico della Marina Militare*, Marzo 2013. PDF.

▲ Sikh destroyer survivors recovered from an Italian boat.

▼ A German minesweeper approaches the docks of the port of Tobruk with British prisoners on board.

▲ From the rescue vehicles, British prisoners have landed on the docks of the port of Tobruk.

▼ British prisoners are removed from the port of Tobruk by vehicle transport.

With the sinking of Coventry, Zulu and the two torpedo boats MTB 308 and MTB 310, the greatest successes were achieved by the German air departments of the X Fliegerkorps and the Fliegerführer Afrika, whose activity can be found on the operational bulletins of the OBB.

The X Fliegerkorps, which is credited with the Ju 88 of the LG.1, the sinking of the cruiser Coventry and the torpedo torch MTB 308, employed ninety-eight Ju 88 throughout the day, of which seventy-five bombers and fourteen scouts, while the Fliegerführer Afrika, whose Stuka sank the Zulu destroyer and the MTB 310 torpedo torch, employed sixteen Ju 88 bombers, seventy-three Ju 87 divers and thirteen Bf 109 fighter-bombers, while another one hundred and three Bf 109 fighters carried out aircraft and alarm departures.

On the Italian side, the Mc 200 fighters of the 13th Assault Group performed very well, which hit the Sikh destroyer with a bomb, destroyed the MTB 312 torpedo-torpedo and the two motor-launches ML 352 and ML 353, and of the 8th Assault Group which they immobilized a second motor torpedo torch, MTB 308, which was later destroyed by a German II./LG.1 plane. Results that, as the commander of the 13th Group, major Viale, wrote in his quoted report, *"were achieved essentially for the courage of the pilots who carried out the shooting in the maximum totality at very low altitude, with serious personal risk for the close explosions of the bombs"*.

Finally, the Sikh destroyer was undoubtedly sunk by the joint efforts of the Italian and German coastal batteries, while the MTB 314 torpedo torpedo was captured unscathed by the Kriegsmarine R 10 minesweeper.

▲ From left, the MTB 313 and MTB 260 Malta. The unit on the right is the MTB 77, which did not participate in the Agreement operation.

All this was achieved with the loss of five German planes, three Ju 88 of II./LG.1, and two divers Ju 87 of II./St.G. 3 collided, and no Italian casualties, while the Allies lost four RAF Wellington bombers and four U.S. B 25 bombers. The destroyer Croone and the ML 354 motor launch were then damaged, and some motor torpedoes with minor damage. As for human losses, 173 men were killed on ships, 64 of them on Coventry, 38 on Zulu; 22 on the Sikh (and 200 men captured), the rest on torpedo boats and motolances.

According to the Diary of the Supreme Command on September 14th, 1942 there were the following Italian-German casualties in Tobruk: 54 dead and 29 injured among the personnel of the Royal Navy and of the San Marco Battalion, 16 dead (1 German) and about 50 injured (7 Germans) among the terrestrial departments.

About the British casualties were counted *"58 dead on land and on naval vessels, as well as very many at sea, and 620 prisoners were made, including over 30 officers[91]"*.

It must be said that in the British failure of the attack on Tobruk, from the moment of the landing until the British retreat, the Germans took most of the merits. Field Marshal Kesselring was the first spokesman, writing to Marshal Ugo Cavallero, Chief of General Staff of the Italian Armed Forces (Supreme Command), on September 17th, arguing that *"Tobruk's failure was due in the front line to the truly superior action of the 114th anti-aircraft reserve group"*. Ultimately, with this statement, Kesselring charged the German cannons the greatest merits for the defense of the square, as well as evidently for the sinking of the Sikh destroyer and the damage to the twin Zulu, as the Germans have always claimed by finding estimators among British historians and researchers.

▲ The loss of the anti-aircraft cruiser Coventry was the most painful for the Royal Navy, also because it deprived the Mediterranean Fleet of a ship that had until then made a significant contribution to the protection of convoys and naval formations. But it was also to be regretted the loss of the two large Sikh and Zulu destroyers.

---

91 Cfr., ASMEUS, Comando Supremo, Sintesi delle operazioni svoltesi in Cirenaica nella notte dal 13 al 14–9–1942-XX, prot. n. 12316 del 18 ottobre 1942.

▲ Unpublished photographs of the British MBT 314 fuel motorbike captured in the port of Tobruk.

This letter, which contained forecasts and judgments on the situation of naval and land traffic on the El Alamein front, and the best way to secure the rear, was read to Benito Mussolini, to whom General Cavallero had said that that of the enemy had *"been a small Dieppe"* (reference to the losses suffered in the British landing on August 20th, 1942) and then sent in copy to Marshal Ettore Bastico, Commander of the Armed Forces of North Africa, on which also Field Marshal Rommel depended. In his reply to Field Marshal Kesselring, regarding the episode of Tobruk Cavallero, probably perplexed, he made no comment, eluding him. On the basis of information received from the commanders of Tobruk and North Africa, Cavallero had had a war report prepared and dictated by the Duce for his approval that same day on September 14th, in which he highlighted, in the enemy failure, the decisive contribution of Italian and German weapons.

▲ On the left, Admiral Giuseppe Lombardi, who organized the counterattack against the landing of the Commandos. For this victory, Lombardi was awarded with the Cross of Knight of the Military Order of Savoy. On the right was lieutenant Giacomo Colotto, who led the Commandos attack and capture the Company Commandos of the San Marco Regiment, about 120 men.

▲ Libya, summer 1942. From left, Field Marshal Erwin Rommel, Commander of the Afrika Battleship Army, Field Marshal Albert Kesselring, Senior Southern Commander (OBS) and Division Admiral Eberhard Weichold, Commander of the German Navy in Italy.

▼ Libya, July 28th, 1942. Marshal Ugo Cavallero talks with Field Marshal Kesselring. They were the two main military personalities who led the destiny of the Axis war in the Mediterranean and North Africa.

CONCLUSIONS

Despite the tactical failures, the "Agreement" operation was not entirely unnecessary for the British. In fact, although it had failed the main purpose of impairing the port of Tobruk, in which the convoys with supplies from Italy and Greece continued to land, starting from September 15th, it obtained the desired result of removing troops from the front El Alamein to protect the rear; and this happened when General Montgomery's 8th Army was preparing the counter-offensive that would bring it, with a deadly shoulder, to the reconquest of western Egypt and an unstoppable advance in Libya and Tunisia. After Alamein, and the landing of Anglo-Americans in French North Africa on November 8th, 1942, the long African campaign ended in just over six months.

At 11:10 on September 14th, in communicating to the Italian Supreme Command the failure of the enemy operation against Tobruk, the Superior Command of the Armored Army Africa (Field Marshal Rommel), providing for *"the repetition of similar attempts to disembark, to oppose them a unitary defense"*, he *"proposed that all the Italian troops in the Tobruk area and east of the same"*, which were under the orders of Marshal Ettore Bastico as Commander in Chief of North Africa, passed under his employ, and ultimately the field marshal Rommel.

This proposal, as was right, did not agree with Marshal Ugo Cavallero, Chief of the General Staff of the Italian Armed Forces. Telegraphing to Tobruk to the North African Delegation (Delase), which was responsible for the logistic organization of landings and movements behind the front lines, proposed to discuss the matter with the German allies. Cavallero, however, put as a firm point the fact that the direction of the defense of the ports and the coastal sector of Cyrenaica had to remain with the Italian Command in Libya (Superlibia), and therefore the responsibility of Marshal Bastico[92]. In fact, the defense of Cyrenaica remained entrusted to the Italian forces, while on the German side a troop battalion was deployed to Sollum. In addition, the Italian infantry division Pavia, under Rommel's orders but with little war efficiency, went on to assume the defense of Marsa Matruh for a few days, while the 90th Germanic motorized division, held in El Daba after the conclusion of the Battle of Halam and Alfa, was also temporarily *"used to defend against possible landings"*[93].

In a report dated October 18th 1942, presented to Marshal Cavallero by the Head of the Operations Office of the Supreme Command, General Antonio Gandin, the subject "Conclusions" was reported verbatim[94]: *The enemy's intention was to destroy the supply bases of our troops operating against the 8th British army. For this purpose he had prepared various combined operations ("Agreement" "Bigamy" "Nicety" - of which the most important was the first against Tobruk - with land, naval and air forces departing from the naval bases of Kaifa and Alerssandria and from the Oasis of Kufra. The preparation must have been long and meticulous; all the details had been studied thoroughly, the various situations that could have arisen had been foreseen; in the orders of operation the dispositions were given for the behavior at all times.*

All operations, however, have completely failed since their inception. The Italian terrestrial, naval and air forces, alone and in harmonious cooperation, managed to contain, beat and repel the opponent causing serious naval and terrestrial losses. German forces of a certain size could only be engaged in the action after 5:30 am.

Flak [anti-aircraft] intervened effectively against naval targets. Our troops all behaved valiantly, resisting in place, intervening promptly, counterattacking. We live the spirit of collaboration, especially between the two Armed Forces - Navy and Army - To which rests the honor and the burden of the fight during the night.

---

92 ASMEUS, Allegato n. 89 al "Diario Cavallero", cartella 1349.
93 Harold. Alexander, *"The African Campaign from El Alamein to Tunis, from 10th August 1942 to 13h May 1943"*, Supplement to the London Gazette of February 13th 1948.
94 AUSMM, "Comando Settore Aeronautico Centrale, Incursione nemica sull'aeroporto di Barce", *Scontri navali e operazioni di guerra*, cartella 91.

The maneuver of a few men and artillery, rationally conducted, has allowed us to achieve maximum results. The action of the Interim Commander of the sector and coordination of the Commander the Tobruk Square is excellent. The action constitutes a brilliant Italian victory.

The Commander of the German Navy in Italy, admiral of division Eberhard Weichold, writing in the immediate post-war period on behalf of the British Admiralty, believed that the plan of the "Agreement" *"was well designed, carefully studying every detail"*; but fortunately for the Axis forces, the purpose of the operation, which could have led to an irreparable damage to the then greater supply port of Cyrenaica, did it because *"the landing of the main department took place in the wrong location. As a result, the north assault group could not begin the attack in just synchrony with the south group, which had advanced through the desert, and it was thus possible to eliminate it before it reached the port fence[95]"*.

Instead, in his judgment on the planning and conduct of the British operation, General Giuseppe Mancinelli wrote[96]: *Of these daring forays of the autonomous departments, it is not known whether the indisputable value and dexterity of the performers or the childish ingenuity of the cumbersome conception of the company should no longer be admired. Thousands of kilometers across the desert hundreds of busy men, planes, ships converging with perfect synchronism on the objectives with the only result of destroying some planes [sic] in Barce, at the price of numerous deaths, hundreds of prisoners, three ships and numerous minor ships sunk . The main action plan on Tobruk, in particular, seems to have come rather from the brain of a detective novel writer than from the operations office of any general staff.*

▲ September 15th, 1942. Field Marshal Rommel flew to Tobruk to personally congratulate the German troops "on their good defensive conduct on the coast". In the picture he praised the pioneers of 5/B.B. 85, who, underestimating what had been the Italians' behaviour, were credited with having made the landing of the British troops fail, while instead they had arrived in the area when the landing had already failed, at 05:30 in the morning of September 14th.

---

95 Eberhard Weichold, *La guerra in Mediterraneo*, USMM, tradotto dall'inglese da Maristat, II Reparto.
96 Annotation of General Giuseppe Mancinelli in the article by R.P. Livinstone, "Le grandi incursioni nel deserto", *Storia della seconda guerra mondiale*, Volume 3, Milano, Rizzoli-Purnell, 1967, p. 311.

▲ German soldiers of Pioneer Company 5/B.B.85 posing on the coast where some survivors of the night landing had been taken prisoner in the raids.

The costly failure of the "Agreement" transaction, of which those who took part in it *"had nothing to be ashamed of"*, and which was charged with *"bad planning and even more ineffective security measures"*, gave rise to London serious apprehensions for the next "Torch" operation, the landing of French North Africa set in early November; and also discontent over the loss of a cruiser, two large destroyers and several soldiers trained in amphibious and command operations. When the report of this failure reached Prime Minister Winston Churchill, the latter being *"known for his proverbial admiration for offensive intentions, he was severely disturbed[97]"*.

But above all the failure, and the losses that resulted from it, so impressed the British commands of the Middle East that, as General Alexander wrote in his report, *"Overland supply lines were no longer attempted of any kind with the exception of some sabotage operations carried out by the Long Range Desert Group against the desert railway[98]"*.

At the same time, however, as mentioned, the vast British action was not entirely useless; because as General Mancinelli wrote, as a final comment on Livingstone's article, making an honest analysis (entirely acceptable for the psychological effect it had especially on Marshals Cavallero and Bastico who feared the repetition of an action similar to the failed one), came to the following conclusions:
"The operation, however, aroused a vigorous alarm in the rear area and undoubtedly had the effect of giving greater evidence to the need to supervise along the very long supply line, from Benghazi to the front, and to strengthen the garrisons in ports and airfields[99]".

Francesco Mattesini

▲ Italian soldiers, protagonists of the Tobruk defence and the failed British landing, were reviewed by Marshal Cavallero and Field Marshal Rommel.

---

97 Stephen Roskill, *The War at Sea 1939-1945*,vol. II, The period of balance, London, HMSO, 1956, p. 310.
98 Harold. Alexander, *"The African Campaign from El Alamein to Tunis, from 10th August 1942 to 13th May 1943"*, Supplement to the London Gazette del 13 febbraio 1948.
99 R.P. Livinstone, "Le grandi incursioni nel deserto", cit., p. 311.

DELLO STESSO AUTORE

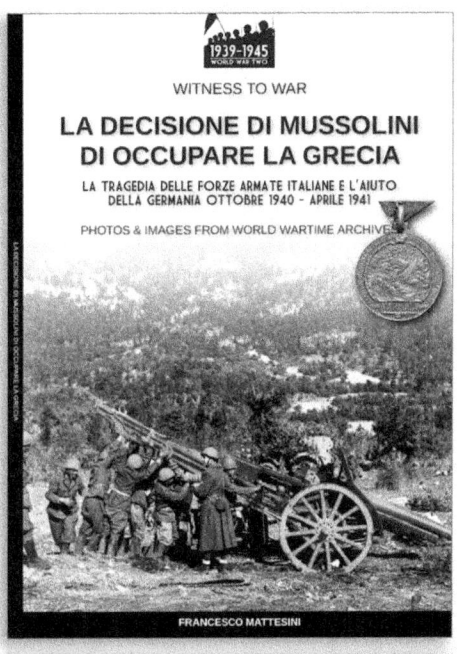

www.ingramcontent.com/pod-product-compliance
Lightning Source LLC
LaVergne TN
LVHW081543070526
838199LV00057B/3760